Voices for Leadership

Your Pathway to Becoming
a More Influential Leader

Brian Brogen

BRIAN BROGEN

1st Edition. 1st printing 2022

Cover Concept and Design: Steve Walters
Interior Design: Steve Walters
Editor: Richard Tardif

Independently Published
Oxygen Publishing Inc.
2515, rue Dutrisac
Vaudreuil-Dorion, QC, Canada J7V 9W7
www.oxygenpublishing.com

ISBN: 978-1-990093-39-5
Imprint: Independently published

Contents

Dedication

To my wife, Jennifer, there is no way I could do anything without your encouragement and support. Words cannot express my gratitude.

To my children, Brittney, James, Matthew and Rebecca, I hope to be a mentor and leader to my family first and foremost. I am pleased with the adults you have become and I am anticipating great things for you in the future.

To all of my mentors and the co-authors of this book, it has been a collaborative effort and I could not have done it without your commitment and support.

Foreword
Larry Levine

If you look back on your day or week or over the last few decades, what you remember are the individual moments that were important to you. I ask you to reflect for a moment. Haven't some of your best leaders impacted your life by creating those moments for you?

I believe we all have times in our life when we are open to new ideas and new ways of thinking. The best leaders understand how to maximize these moments to change the course of our future.

I am reminded of this quote by psychologist Ellen Langer, "Life consists only of moments, nothing more than that. So if you make the moment matter, it all matters."

Leaders look for those rare opportunities when they don't have to fight through the clutter to help us understand things. In today's crazy-busy business world, there are not enough leaders, not enough leadership, and not enough who lead and influence from the heart.

There is an age-old saying, "Birds of a feather flock together." Apply this to leadership, which means heartfelt and influential leaders associate with one another.

We live in an interconnected world. We all are one degree of separation from someone who can impact our life.

That being said, Brian Brogen and I connected through LinkedIn on June 17, 2020. Life is about moments. At that moment, neither of us realized our impact on each other and our journey.

On October 6, 2020, I had the privilege of being on Brian's *Build Your Success Podcast.* After we finished recording, Brian and I engaged in small talk, and then inquisitively, Brian asked, "What would you do to enhance the show or change the flow of the podcast?"

Memorable moments will forever alter life's journey. I shared with Brian the flow of my podcast, *Selling From the Heart,* that we create a signature question moment at the beginning of every podcast to ask every guest. "What does it mean to you to sell from the heart?"

I asked Brian, "What does leadership and being a leader mean to you?"

At that moment, Brian and I connected. Connecting with others is a true leadership gift. As a leader, are you connecting with those you serve?

As you read *Voices for Leadership,* look inward and reflect on the following questions:

- Am I encouraging others to become the best version of themselves?

- Am I making myself available to serve?

- Am I faithful and trustworthy?

- Am I present in my conversations with others?

Leadership is a gift. It's the gift of compassion, kindness, and heartfelt caring for others.

A heartfelt leader commits and connects to serving others. They walk, talk, live, and breathe every aspect of servanthood.

Leaders use their voice, their words, and their message to influence the lives of others.

To quote Pastor Craig Groeschel, "You have no idea how one conversation, one word of encouragement or one expression of love might change someone's life."

As a leader, I will ask you, "How are you using your influence?" Influence isn't always obvious and isn't always instant. Because you didn't see the harvest doesn't mean the seed didn't take root.

My dear friend, coach and mentor, Dave Sanderson, always stressed to me, "All the moments in your life do matter. You never know which moments will make a real difference."

Apply what you learn from these amazing authors to transform your relationships with others; isn't this what you crave?

Larry Levine

Author of Selling *From the heart: How your authentic self sells you.*

BRIAN BROGEN

Introduction

My name is Brian Brogen. I am the founding author of the Voices For Leadership series. Before I introduce this book and our community, I want to give you a little background about myself and my leadership journey.

As a teenager, my parents divorced, and I made poor choices that led to spending some time in a troubled youth's home. I bounced back and forth between my parents, attending five different high schools. I struggled in high school and barely graduated with a few credits through community service.

After graduation, I was looking for a job and stumbled upon a gratifying career in construction. This career has led to tremendous opportunities to volunteer as a board member in a local construction users' group and mentor high school students. Not only do I get to encourage young people to consider construction as a career, but I also try to help them connect education to industry.

As a high school student, I never connected what I was learning to a career. As a mentor, I use real-world examples to encourage young people to take advantage of their education.

Now that I have been a mentor for several years and have seen the development of young people, I have discovered that I am passionate about helping others grow and develop themselves. I now build buildings and development projects, but I also build up professionals and help them develop. In June 2019, I became the host of *The Build Your Success Podcast*.

As the host of *The Build Your Success Podcast*, I have met some amazing leaders, learned many lessons and created friendships. I have interviewed over 100 unique leaders from across the globe, creating entertaining and insightful conversations.

One guest was Larry Levine, the author of *Selling From the Heart*. Larry is very engaging, with a passion for the sales profession and sales leaders. At the end of my interviews, I like to ask my guests, "How can I improve the podcast?" Larry was complimentary about the flow of the discussion and the quality of my questions, although he offered one suggestion. "Brian, consider creating a signature question for your podcast? We have a signature question based on sales for our podcast. You should develop a question about leadership that is asked of all your guests."

Larry and I went back and forth with a few emails and settled on this question: "What does leadership and being a leader mean to you?" I have asked this question of many leaders. The answers have been unique and have led me to understand that leadership, like success, is defined differently by different people from diverse backgrounds.

This question and the answers have led to the Voices For Leadership community and this book series.

I hope you enjoy this book and join our community. I have written below the allegory of the *Sea of Leadership* to welcome you aboard.

The sea of leadership

You and I are in a vast sea of leadership.

It is a beautiful sea, with lovely sunsets and beautiful creatures. We can enjoy the sounds of waves crashing and birds singing.

We reminisce about the day we left the shore. There were hundreds, if not thousands of other leaders beginning their journey into the sea. We gathered on the shore to inspire and encourage one another. We chanted together with messages of hope.

We seldom see those other rafts. Some have suffered shipwrecks at sea. Occasionally, we will pass another raft, only to be separated again by the shifting sea.

The sea of leadership has been good to us. It has provided our food and a way to convey our rafts on our journey. We have learned to navigate obstacles and celebrate opportunities.

However, the sea can sometimes be lonely, and when the waves turn boisterous they can be frightening. Your raft sinks between the tall waves and the howling winds, and crashing thunder bombards your ears. As the sea settles and you take a breath of the calm and fresh salty air, you see ferocious sharks circling your raft. Your heart pounds again, and you wish your vessel was more substantial.

On the sea, your voice is an echo. The sea's vastness devours your voice as if no one is listening.

And then, as if from nowhere, a ship appears on the horizon. At first, you think it's a mirage. Then you hear someone calling in the distance.

As the ship gets closer, you see many leaders like you, some a little damp from being picked up from the sea a few miles ago. Others have been aboard a little longer and smile as they let down the rope ladder, and invite you to join a group of leaders who want to share in the journey.

You are excited to join, yet hesitant to abandon the raft that has carried you through the storms. It is then you realize they built the ship using other rafts like yours. In fact, every time someone boards, the vessel becomes stronger and grows larger.

This ship will provide conveniences not available on the raft, such as prepared food and shelter, and a community to encourage and inspire each other. This is a place to call home. Welcome aboard the *SS Voices For Leadership*.

This book is broken down into four Pillars of Leadership. These pillars have been foundational and transformational for the authors of this book.

Purpose

Your why; what motivates and inspires you to be a leader?

Leadership

Guiding principles to be an influential leader
in the lives of others.

Communication

Learning to communicate with clarity
and hearing the needs of others.

Mentorship

Modeling leadership and developing potential in others.

**Find out more about our authors and community @
voicesforleadership.com**

Purpose

Your why; what motivates and inspires you to be a leader?

How to lead through the storms of life and turn setbacks into incredible comebacks

By Dr. Willie Jolley

Featured author
Washington, D.C.

Over the last year, we have been through a series of setbacks: A global pandemic, economic downturn, massive job losses, racial strife, and social upheaval. I am here to proclaim that it is "comeback time."

If you're an entrepreneur, you must keep in mind that setbacks happen to all of us—even the many successful entrepreneurs. The primary determining factor in the outcome will be how you handle it. If you sit back and let your problems bury you and leave it at that, then you might as well put up the tombstone and let your dreams rest in peace. But if you change your perspective, don't get flustered, and see your setbacks as setups for comebacks; you can change course and build your way up again and win.

For setbacks in business, here are six things to remember.

1. Decide if you see this as a setback, period, or a setback, comma: We all learn two important punctuations that affect what we read in

elementary school, a period and a comma. A period means the end of the story, but a comma means to pause; more to come. You must decide if this setback is the end of your story or a pause, a transition; there is more to come. Plus, that thinking helps you come to a place where you see this setback as not the end of the road, but a bend. For example, do we change/pivot or stick our heads in the ground and do nothing during the pandemic?

2. Don't wait for your ship to come in: One of the core values of your work ethic should be to go out and create opportunities. Don't wait for them to fall from the sky neatly gift-wrapped into your lap. You need to be relentless and constantly find new ways to expand and refine your business. If you feel as though you are struggling, reassess your business's weakest points and then think about how you can fix them. You'll have to look at yourself objectively and honestly, and determine what needs improvement. Be professional yet aggressive, and reach out toward any opportunity that can help your business grow. You need to build your ship. If you wait for one to come along, you'll simply be treading water, and eventually, sink.

3. Never stop learning: You know all of those professional development courses and self-improvement seminars and books? They serve an important purpose. If you keep doing things the same way, you will get the same results. Being successful in anything, but especially in business, means never stop learning and dedicating yourself to being open to new ways of thinking and doing things. This is especially important when facing a setback. Instead of falling victim, you'll be full of strategies to change your outcome and get you back on the road to success.

4. You haven't tried this: I'll speak to someone going through a setback in their business, and they'll tell me they have tried everything. But when I ask, "Have you tried this or that," the answer is, "I never thought of that." So, you realize you haven't tried everything but have tried the things you thought of initially. You must keep thinking. So, here is

an exercise to help. First, list all the ways you can turn your setback around. Once you have exhausted your list, ask those in your network for their ideas. It will amaze you at what they come up with. There is always another way that you didn't think about to take on your current problem. So, keep thinking.

5. Speak positivity into your business: Even when things have hit a rough spot or business is slow, you must speak positivity into your business and life. Your language directly affects your mindset and how life will respond to your situation. Amid a setback, it's easy to beat yourself up and become negative. If you find your thoughts like, "I am desperate for work. I don't know if I will make it. Maybe I should hang up the towel," change it to, "I am an expert and very good at what I do. I do occasionally have some challenges, but so does everyone, and they are always temporary. I'm going to bounce back." Remember, what you speak is what you attract.

6. Never give up: This is the golden rule of entrepreneurship. Any success that you've ever heard of, whether it be the great captains of industry, multinational corporations, or even entire nations, have faced setbacks, some of which seemed insurmountable. Many learned from it and went on to greater success than they had hoped for. You can do the same. You may feel you've lost everything, and you've reached the end. That's usually far from the truth. Never, ever, give up.

When you encounter a setback, you need to move forward. Being disappointed after something goes wrong is natural, but letting that feeling take over will accomplish nothing but failure. In the end, it's up to you. Remember, a setback is nothing but a setup for a comeback.

I have lots of eagles in my office to remind me to be like an eagle, and not like an ostrich. In times of storms, the ostrich will stick its head in the ground and say, "Let me know when it is over." Yet, the eagle does something strange. During the storm, the eagle takes flight and flies right into the face of the storm. It fights through the storm, persists, and perseveres, and eventually gets above the storm and gets a panoramic view of the situation. The eagle sees a serious problem at a specific place, but then the eagle looks up the road and realizes that, "It is good further up the road." The lesson? Do not stop now! There is good further up the road. This setback is nothing but a setup for an amazing comeback, and it is now COMEBACK TIME.

So fly high.

Face: The ancient tool for modern connection

By Maya Hu-Chan

Featured author
Powa, California

Our modern business world is complex, but it pays to get back to the basics of human connection for effective leadership. Strong leaders are agile. They can connect to a diversity of people on an individual, fundamental level. An understanding of "face" helps make this possible.

In Chinese culture, the concept of "face" has been central to understanding human relationships for over 3,000 years. Face refers to an individual's sense of dignity, self-esteem, and respect. We lose some of that dignity when we "lose face" (a Chinese idiom that has become part of the American lexicon). When we "save face," we recover it. To "honor face" is to help someone build it.

Friction in business relationships is the result of lost face—or a lack of honoring "face." When leaders are sensitive to these dynamics, they can navigate these situations more adeptly.

I worked with a tech company to help its leaders figure out why a relationship with a vendor had soured. The company partnered with this vendor to design and produce products that ultimately go to market. The partnership requires working hand in hand to collaborate and make joint decisions.

The relationship started strongly but deteriorated. Workers on the vendor side started asking for assignments with other clients. After a series of feedback interviews with people on both the company and vendor sides, one thing became obvious: The breakdown was all about "face."

Here's how "face" was lost, saved, and built, and what all leaders can learn from their experience.

"Where did you go to school?"

When I spoke to workers on the vendor side, they reported feeling a clear one-up/one-down relationship, not an equal partnership. When setbacks occurred, they didn't work hand in hand with the tech company to brainstorm solutions. Instead, people pointed fingers and assigned blame at bi-weekly status meetings, in full view of other colleagues. Project managers asked engineers on the vendor side questions such as, "Where did you go to school? Didn't they teach you how to [do a specific thing]?"

The public blaming caused the engineers to lose face. They felt ashamed and humiliated and felt they had lost all credibility. Someone would instead transfer them to another client rather than to lose face again.

"Done. Next project."

Several senior leaders on the vendor side reported feeling unappreciated. Their teams put in long, arduous hours to complete projects on deadline, but never received recognition or shown gratitude for their work. One leader said their partnership felt transactional. "All we get is, 'Done. Next project.'"

Expressing sincere appreciation is one way to honor "face." Because the tech company didn't thank the vendor teams for their hard work, they felt unappreciated in their contributions. It deprived them of an essential gesture of respect.

"Our bar is high."

When I interviewed people from the tech company, I discovered they were not bad people. They had good intentions. From their point of view, the status meetings were not about finger-pointing—they were asserting their company's high standards. "Our bar is high. When we see things that don't meet our quality standards, we have to question their judgment."

I'm coaching the tech company's leaders to view feedback through the lens of "face." It does not mean abandoning the company's high standard—it means keeping the vendor team's sense of dignity at the forefront. Critical feedback should be delivered but privately and respectfully. I also invited them to think of "face" as currency. By expressing appreciation for the team's hard work, they are building enough deposits of "face" to cover for the withdrawals of critical feedback.

"What can be done to strengthen the partnership?"

My feedback interviews revealed both parties contributed to the deterioration of their relationship. The vendor was not wholly blameless—they had made their errors, particularly in failing to communicate across their cross-functional teams, which led to repeated mistakes that frustrated the tech company.

I asked both parties for recommended solutions, and each side rattled off lists of suggestions, but not for them, for the other party. When I asked, "Are there any things your company needs to do?"

Silence.

Growth requires the humility to look in the mirror and ask, what can I do differently? Once each party could do that, they started offering concrete suggestions. And by sharing them—and acting on them—they mended their relationship. Each time one party took ownership of a past misstep they regained the trust of the other. They honored "face."

Face is an ancient concept with timeless, universal relevance because it speaks to essential human needs, appreciation and respect. These needs are as relevant on a virtual call today as they were face to face 3,000 years ago.

When building relationships with colleagues, team members, and clients, keep their dignity and respect at the forefront. Minimize opportunities for lost face and maximize opportunities to honor face. Make "face" important, and you will always create strong human connections.

What do you believe about your voice for leadership?

By Melahni Ake

Indianapolis, Indiana

In every person's life, there comes a time to reflect on circumstances that have had significant impacts on understanding how to navigate the future.

You may read this and remember the one person who at the right moment gave you a word of encouragement, a sense of confidence, or a borrowed belief about who you were or how you should fit into the world. It may even feel like others could see things about you and your purpose in life before you could. Do you remember a time in your life when this happened? Have you taken time to track back the significance of borrowing that belief? My mentor, Dr. John Maxwell, has taught me the value of evaluated reflection and how this important part is a catalyst to transformational personal growth.

In 1970, I was two years old, and my family lived on the property of my great grandparents' Evangelistic Center in Indianapolis, Indiana. My great-grandfather, Reverend Elwood Patton Qualls, came to Indianapolis in the early 1940s from the Pilgrims Holiness Church in Portsmouth, Ohio.

His goal was to build his vision, a vision that would provide faith-based community resources including but not limited to, a worship tabernacle, school, retirement housing and nursing home. My environment, family history, and the borrowed beliefs of others influenced me. As a young child in the development years, these are your core. This shapes your mind to form relationships, choose careers, and ultimately learn how to develop your gifts to reach your potential. As I trace my memories and my life back to these moments, I can close my eyes and hear the voices of my family. I can distinctly hear my great-grandfather's powerful voice leading from his tabernacle pulpit, teaching and influencing others around him who were searching for their beliefs. Listening to his words would influence them to be courageous.

My grandparents, Paul Matthew Qualls and Mae McKinney Qualls, were an important part of the Evangelistic Center because they were song evangelists in their professional calling, and contributed to the ministry at the tabernacle through their gift of music. My grandfather had a beautifully rich and deep baritone voice which allowed him to become a sought-after song evangelist, and my grandmother faithfully accompanied him as a singer and pianist. My grandparents spent their lives equipping others and sharing their beliefs through their voices. Often, I reflect on the camp meetings I attended every summer and the minister's messages that have affected my life. I remember my grandfather sharing a story from the pulpit, recalling how his voice was such a gift, and how he understood that God had designed him with a purpose to inspire others and bring them to Christ.

He said, "I don't understand why people want to sing about anything other than Jesus." My grandfather was my greatest inspiration; to use your voice to stand for what you believe in. His message was simple: "Don't show up or compare yourself or your gifts to anyone else in the world, use your gifts and your heart to serve others."

How often could we gain more influence as leaders if we could use our voice to create a bigger impact on our lives and for our communities? What if we could intentionally use our voice to lead our lives to serve others with a bigger vision that can identify our real needs?

My mentor says, "Motivation gets you going, but discipline keeps you growing," and over the last 10 years, I have spent thousands of hours focusing on personal development to add value to myself and to others. I've stayed curious and creative to ensure I was gaining momentum. As I turned 50, it was critical to add self-value and value to others, so I started an evaluation process to understand what had impacted my life, what I saw for the next stage of my life, and how to blend these together. Clarity kicked in, and I immediately knew what to do to celebrate those who have impacted my life. My grandparents were 50 years old when I was born, and I knew that without their influence, I would have not developed my beliefs or the courage to sustain them.

I combined my passion and training in broadcast journalism through the *Everyday Leaders Podcast*. My vision was to create a space to celebrate people like my grandparents, who used their voices to overcome obstacles and create inspiration in others.

Everyday Leaders has hosted hundreds of guests, creating collaborations, live events, workshops and daily leadership devotionals. Our voice matters in every moment. Only when we learn how to lead can we effectively learn how to lead others. Everyday leaders can change the world.

How are you committing your life to use your voice to impact leadership?

Removing the K factor from your success

By Enrique Acosta Gonzalez
Orlando, Florida

The stage

Maybe you're a person who wants to be a leader? Or you have already led people at your job, church, school, or at home? In leadership, your decisions lead to amounts of success, and are tied to the lives of many people.

I want to introduce you to K factors and where they show up to hamper your success.

Introduction to K factors

K factors are things you cannot easily identify. They make their way into your ability to be successful, to achieve your goals. K factors hinder you from achieving genuine success. It is the silent killer to many leaders and their effectiveness. Until you are truthful about your condition, you will battle these factors and might derail your career or someone else's.

There are six areas where K factors will show up in your leadership, and you must be honest and ready to deal with them when they do.

You

The main actor in the play of your life is you. K factors have been brewing in you since you started processing thoughts and verbalizing words. They have seeped in through the many teachings throughout your life. K factors are subtle but deadly in action, but do not produce immediate repercussions. Your ability to execute success starts within you.

It could be a lazy way you handle issues, an indifference toward a task at hand, or a lack of motivation. We all have K factors, but the key is to identify these areas in our lives in private, and in an honest exploration so that we do not become the reason we fail. If anyone gives you an opportunity, it should be you. Look at yourself and address those K factor areas for your best shot at success.

Talent

Once you tackle your K factors, investigate your talent toolbox. Many of us can do different things, but we focus on one thing we do great. Talent requires many dedicated hours of practice and execution to stand out from the crowd. We must invest in honing our crafts and getting better over time.

I encourage you to dig into your toolbox, see what you have at your disposal, and lay them out on a table. Collaborate with a person who has the talent you are missing ,or add a new skill. K factors come into play when you think you can get by with the wrong tool because you can still use it, and it can get the job done eventually. Do not let K factors invade your talent toolbox.

Timing

Time is something we cannot control. Many of us have hit or missed the attempts at managing time. K factors derail your attempts at time management through time sappers like the Internet, television, and social media platforms. We are given the same time, but we do not handle time the same.

Take a moment and look at how you handle time from when you wake until you sleep. Make an inventory of your activities and those things you allow to sap your time. If you want success to reign in your life, identify K factors immediately and respond so that you can begin appropriating the time you need to execute your life goals and plans.

Environment

K factors do best by roaming around looking for a suitable environment. It inserts itself into suitable settings, bustling with people. Your environment is as important to success as any other element. The water fountain conversation is not the problem; the issue arises when the conversation takes on a certain tone or does not promote good order, off ramping you from the leadership lanes.

You may remember something not being right, a feeling in your gut that the conversation or surroundings were off. You have now identified a K factor arriving. The decision you take now will determine its impact on your leadership ability and reputation.

Mission

We endeavor to find our purpose, and as leaders, help others find their purpose. We create mission statements that guide us on the journey, and give us course corrections along the way, leading to our ultimate success. K factors insert themselves into your mission statements by injecting daily routine activities that do not feed your mission goals. They show up as activities that seem like they could help but never support your mission, and therefore strip you of valuable actions that could. The goal of K factors is to keep you busy and unproductive.

Results

How can you have things in order and still fail? K factors like to surprise you; they reveal themselves in the unexpected results. Then, we hurry to find how this could happen, who is responsible, or why us?

What can you do when K factors have their way with you? I choose to look at myself, employ laughter, and think, "What can I learn from this moment to help me get back on track?" Things will not be perfect; learn how to laugh and get on with life. It will be smoother and you will give those K factors less time in the spotlight.

Ten leadership reasons diversity, equity & inclusion efforts fail

By Hayward L. Bell
Waltham, Massachusetts

W hat does diversity, equity & inclusion (DEI) have to do with leadership? Everything!

We expect leaders to get the most from the people they lead. A distinguishing feature of outstanding leaders is their ability to attract and coalesce a diverse group of talented people who will give their maximum contribution to a mission.

Doing so requires DEI skills and competence.

10. Public relations is the primary reason for your DEI effort

It is valuable to build, protect, and enhance the public image of your organization. However, DEI as a public relations stunt is backwards and worse, damaging. DEI done effectively will improve morale, increase employee engagement and retention, enhance customer experience and increase innovation, resulting in stronger brands and company image. If however, there is a gap between your external appearance and the internal reality, this incongruence will be long-lasting and hurt your credibility.

9. IQ Sickness - Leaders cannot focus on themself and their contribution to the problem and solution

Senior leaders have high levels of education, experience, and are recognized and sought-after in their discipline or industry. Their organization may enjoy success. Hence, leaders conclude that they need not spend time and effort on diversity education and development. This posture is problematic because gaining diversity, understanding, and competence is a lifelong journey. It usually starts with re-visiting what you have been taught and re-examining beliefs you hold dear. This ongoing work is arduous for everyone, especially highly intelligent people, who have enjoyed success based on their existing beliefs and points of view. As a senior leader, you must model the inclusive behavior you want to see in your organization.

8. Lack of DEI functional competence

Frequently, accomplished and respected leaders in an organization are appointed to lead DEI efforts without the necessary education, development, and experience. Being intelligent and accomplished is valuable, but insufficient for becoming a grounded strategic diversity leader. This role requires a deep understanding of diversity concepts, including cultural competence, understanding and experience leading change, and a commitment to ongoing personal development. It does not suggest that an accomplished business leader cannot be appointed to the role, especially if they have experience in the business and organizational credibility. Still, they must commit themselves to DEI development while they leverage their experience and credibility.

7. Delegating accountability for DEI

For the long, arduous DEI journey, you need the commitment of the senior leaders. Too often, accountability for diversity progress is delegated down into the organization, to people who do not have the power or influence to change the culture or systems to sustain improvement. In the best case, DEI will be on the CEO's short-list, and even then, the work is challenging and is resisted.

6. Cultural critical success factors are not understood and addressed

Diversity improvement is about change, systems, and culture. The traditional tactics used in DEI (e.g. employee groups, councils, etc.), usually require cultural adjustments or accommodations, so they work. They implement programs and processes without understanding the culture necessary to support them. As we know, culture eats strategy for lunch. Ignoring cultural nuances will doom your effort, especially globally.

5. Quick fix mentality

In organizations, speed is king. In publicly traded companies, the focus on quarterly results, fiscal year budgets, annual incentive plans, etc., drive scrutiny and the need for quick turnaround. Changing systems and culture as part of DEI takes time. The constant pressure for short-term DEI results can cause organizations to take counter-productive actions to sustain improvement. The partial remedy is a strategic diversity plan that includes short, medium and long-term wins. It may not satisfy the hyper type A organization, which is another reason solid CEO commitment, not lip service, is required.

4. DEI is not integrated with the organization's strategy and operations

Organizations have limited resources, time constraints and multiple headwinds. Only the high priority efforts will be supported and sustained. If DEI is not integrated into the strategic thrusts, it will be sacrificed when the headwinds blow. Elements of a business strategy are not only emphasized; they are deeply understood. Within this context, the value proposition for DEI will generate commitment and action.

3. Little or no accountability

Think of culture as behavior that is expected, reinforced and rewarded. We must establish accountability for DEI results at all levels of management. Accountability includes metrics, performance objectives, compensation, and assignments/promotions. Often, establishing DEI accountability will create dilemmas we must prepare the organization to deal with, such as when the top historic performers fail to meet their DEI deliverables. Accountability is a classic "walk the talk" acid test.

2. Lack of or inadequate resources

DEI work includes educating and developing leaders to build their diversity competence, and assessing internal systems and processes to create a culture of inclusion. This significant long-term effort requires time and resources. Appointing a CDO (Chief Diversity Officer), no matter how competent, is woefully inadequate without resources. That person must have access to internal and external resources, and the time and attention of senior leaders. Failure to provide adequate resources will doom the DEI effort. An article in the Financial Times, The Evolution of the Chief Diversity Officer, in September 2021, by Emma Jacobs, said, "The title is meaningless if an organization's head of diversity has little sway, budget or clarity of purpose."

1. Lack of understanding of the DEI Initiative

Employee groups, diversity councils, diversity training, diversity conferences, diversity awards, mentoring, sponsorship programs, and targeted recruiting are tactics but are not themselves the DEI initiative. The work is systems and culture change. The initiative requires re-education, development, increased competency, and ongoing vigilance. DEI deals with human dilemmas and contradictions, and requires addressing them in a robust change plan and strategy fully supported and resourced by management. While these tools and techniques may be employed, the key test is, do they deliver and sustainably increase employee engagement and higher levels of productivity and innovation?

Sustaining improvement in DEI is a complex adaptive problem versus a technical issue, primarily because of human dynamics. The standard tools and approaches do not work in every situation. We must adapt most of them according to the phase of the change process.

A good example is diversity training, which inevitably fails. Diversity competence requires education, skill-building, follow-up, and practice. Assessment should precede diversity competence. Sometimes, it requires un-learning and recalibration.

A Harvard Business Review article in August 2016 suggested the positive effects of diversity training rarely last beyond a day or two. This is because the "training" is not connected to a longer-term education process that supports building competency, and improving the results of individuals, teams and leaders; or because, as pointed out, a need to react to lawsuits and financial settlements drives diversity training.

You as a leader must be intentional and have clarity of the purpose of your DEI goals. A true DEI program is a culture changing commitment that will expand your team and their capacity.

Choose to be a great leader

By Mikel Bowman
Bloomington, Indiana

I was once told by the president of an organization I worked for, "Mikel, there's two kinds of leaders in this old world."

1. The leader stands looking over the field of battle. His men are all behind him. The moment he sounds the charge, and the horn blows, all of his warriors run ahead, so their King doesn't get hurt because he's so beloved.

2. The leader stands proud, scowling over the field of battle and full of himself, knowing he is King. And as King, his rule is absolute. The moment he sounds the charge and the horn of war blows, all of his men take twelve steps back, hoping the King is the first to die.

This statement had such a lasting and profound impact on me. At that moment, I heard a voice in my head say, "Which one of those do you want to be? The choice is entirely up to you, Mikel."

For me, there was no question who I wanted to be. I end all my posts with this saying, "Build a legacy that will far surpass your legend." This means that

I want to lead and live in such a way that makes the ultimate impact. I want my deeds and intentions to live on in others I share life with, long after I am forgotten.

My friend, I am asking you the following:

1. Which leader do you want to be?

2. Which of the two leaders do you think you are?

3. Last, of the people you lead, which one of those leaders do they think you are?

Who do you want to be?

The difference between being a great leader or someone who manages groups of people toward a common goal are two completely different things.

It's like the adage, "All because you are standing in a garage doesn't make you a car." The same is true of leadership. All because you may be the head of your family, president of the company, CEO, project manager, business owner, or an influencer (and the list goes on) doesn't make you a great leader. Your title, my friend, means little if you cannot lead at a high level.

The more and more I looked at my desire to become a great leader and measured myself up to my boss' statement, I realized the first step was to ask myself, who did I want to be? What kind of role as a leader did I desire for myself? And to do that, I had to define the type of leader I wanted to aspire to.

Oh sure, I wanted to be the sort of leader whose troops all charged ahead. I could ask who in history did that and what attributes I need to emulate?

Of course, I could regale about the thousands of years of great leaders in history that made all the difference in battles, business, or professional sports. However I looked to a leader that made all the difference in the world to me.

His name was Perry. He was understanding, caring, and intentional about how he approached me. Perry honored me regularly, celebrating when I did things right and patiently guiding me along the way when I made missteps. In his continued effort to help me become a better leader, he never flinched and helped me hone my craft, no matter how bad he felt or how much he had on his plate.

Perry is who I wanted to be because of his resolute approach and continued commitment to seeing that I moved forward. I would have, and still to this day charge ahead of Perry, knowing his value as a leader is far greater than mine.

Who do you think you are?

So often, we are mistakenly sure of the leader we see in the mirror. If we are not careful and our ego goes unchecked, we can quickly lead our families and businesses astray.

The inverse can be true as well. We can have such doubt and self-loathing that we second guess ourselves and miss seizing great opportunities for our team, family, and business.

Balance, my friend, is what you need. Ushering balance into your life, looking crystal clear in your approach, measuring yourself to the leader you want to be are all vital to growing as a leader. Measuring out your motives, reasons, and being honest with yourself will give you the type of followers, workers, teammates, and family that consistently win.

Who do those you lead think you are?

Too many leaders never ask, "How am I doing?" to those they lead. This is such a disappointing thing to me, especially in the family setting. When leaders don't ask those who follow them this question, they are frightened by what they will hear or simply don't care. I challenge you to do this. You can adjust missteps or forge ahead, knowing you are doing a great job.

Leading in this way is without a doubt where you as a leader humble yourself enough to hear and listen, that produces the greatest impact on those validating their opinions of you. When you, the one who is ultimately responsible for the whole, bow to those you lead and take complete ownership over your actions, you shift the mood and culture of others to want to do the same.

When you lead in this manner, and the battle horn blows, your warriors will charge ahead to protect you. And this way, my friend, you will undoubtedly become a great leader and build a legacy that will far surpass your legend.

Courage to lead

By Glenn Gonzales

Greensboro, North Carolina

Throughout history and folklore, we portray heroes as standing alone in a blaze of fire, victorious over insurmountable odds. In the fairytale, *Sleeping Beauty*, the dragon, determined to prevent a life filled with love, peace and prosperity, is slain by the fearless Prince Phillip. Heroes are glorified in 20 minutes or less from challenges enveloped in fast cutting scenes, rising orchestral crescendos, and flirtations with death of which success can only result from divine intervention.

These portrayals are easily relatable, but rarely is the life of a hero so simple. Seldom is the journey to a moment of victory encapsulated in a 90 minute story. Never does the hand of fate singularly direct our destiny. The courage to lead is an attribute that is earned through trial by fire. It is the toll booth that every successful individual must pass. Any successful leader must have the courage to lead.

The courage to lead is a lonely rite of passage practiced before the stakes are highest. General Douglas MacArthur stated, "Upon the fields of friendly strife are sown the seeds that on other days, on other fields, will bear the fruits of victory."

Consistent practice and training build courage. By embarking on the road less traveled, few people surround leaders. Comparing a new business, which hires the best talent it can afford and works to do more with less, to an established company that employs superior talent into overstaffed divisions, shows this norm.

In either case, the courage to lead recognizes that one's path is one of solitude that is guided by an internal purpose. My journey of transitioning from flying fighters in the US Air Force to building one of the fastest-growing private jet companies in the world is an example of this evolution.

As an overconfident and naïve teenager from Houston, Texas, I entered the United States Air Force Academy focused on playing Division I basketball and becoming an Air Force fighter pilot. I immediately questioned my decision when a screaming upper class cadet insisted I must cut my milk soaked Cheerios in half before eating!

The constant verbal and physical training experienced during my Doolie (freshman) year was terribly lonely. The months of isolation from my family and hometown friends took its toll on me physically, and the stress resulted in frequent ailments. However, courage fueled my determination, and I fought through loneliness, physical exhaustion, and mental anguish to earn my purpose of attending. Eventually, I served as the Men's basketball team captain and later became an F-15C fighter pilot. The Academy was my introduction to the courage to lead.

After a decade of flying supersonic aircraft, I left the Air Force in the middle of a global recession. Traditionally, military pilots transition from war-fighting cockpits to commercial airlines. Contrary to the norm, I selected a career in private aviation. My peers and mentors challenged my decision through a lens of confusion and doubt. Their skepticism quickly became internal when I found myself unemployed with two toddlers and a spouse two months into the decision. This early setback was an ego-bruising and emotionally painful experience, considering I left a comfortable military career and ignored a lucrative airline pilot job to navigate an uncharted course. For months, the agony of my situation became lonelier until I received a call to return to private aviation. I based the courage to double down in the face of ridicule on a new vision. I would transition from the cockpit to CEO.

These few months of my story are far from the dramatization of leadership in movies. Successful organizations have leaders who are champions in situations that take place beyond the spotlight of glory. They have leaders who champion bad ideas as forcefully as they pursue winning ideas. They are essential to any organizational success, and although the path begins lonely, it changes as others recognize the courage, competency, character, and commitment of the individual leading the way. Others follow the path because of the ideals we find in our storybooks; love, family and prosperity are common ideals among all humans. When vision directed actions align with personal values, it becomes easy to follow.

The courage to lead is universal, and each person embarks upon their dragon slaying journey, building courage one trial at a time. According to Paulo Coelho, in *The Alchemist*, "Courage is the quality most essential to understanding the language of the world."

The everyday leader understands the world's language to be the importance of every moment in time and how it leads into the next. Those with the courage to lead create the goals they seek. They are selective in who is included on their journey and why. They have a habit of recognizing what may be around the corner and preparing for it; the athlete who consistently performs in the clutch moments of the game and the musician who performs flawlessly on their orchestral debut do so because they prepared for the moment. They have spent countless lonely hours practicing for the opportunity to arise, with expected results.

For these individuals, the pounding heart and rising crescendos become a brief nervousness that quickly fades as the courage to lead kicks in. What begins as a singular vision that challenges the status quo becomes an inevitable moment. It is not fate that creates the moment, but awareness that if one plays in enough games, they will eventually find themselves in a position to take the last shot or slay their life's dragon. When one has the courage to lead, others will follow.

Overcoming life mistakes and rediscovering your passion along the way

By Stephanie Hoskins

Lakeland, Florida

I tried to die. Several times. Half of me lived to succeed, seeking the approval and recognition of peers and my supervisors. The other half of me couldn't stand the fact that I wasn't reaching the goals I had set for myself, no matter how unrealistic they may or may not have been.

Having once been an elite athlete swimmer for an NCAA Division I team, I knew what it took to win and achieve. As a child, I was disciplined to reach the lofty goal of swimming in college on an athletic scholarship. My mother's dream had been answered. She couldn't afford to pay for my college education. I found a field of study I enjoyed and balanced swimming, a part-time job, and social life.

After graduating, something happened; I was thrust into adulthood with no structure.

I moved home, found an entry-level crap job pushing papers across a desk I shared with a cantankerous "old" lady who didn't like me. It was awful. I tried my hardest to fit in, become an adult, conform to the culture, learn, excel, and even thrive. But the little voice inside me kept saying, you're not winning. You're not reaching some crazy level of unknown success you've set for yourself.

The funny thing is when highly successful athletes or artists have to retire they don't know what to do with themselves. They find bad habits quickly over the more positive ones. I drank. I had never touched alcohol until I was 19. Of course, I drank a bit during college, but this wasn't drinking at a college frat party type drinking. I would saddle up, alone, at this terribly scuzzy hole in the wall, grease slick with dingy windows, a cigarette machine, and not nearly enough oxygen in the room to improve the chances for good decisions.

The bartender's name was Lana. She would pour an 11-ounce shot of vodka into a glass with a quick hit of seltzer. Four days a week, I'd get there shortly after leaving work and leave when Lana turned the lights off. I didn't go shopping. I didn't make friends. I drank.

I worked. Then I worked so I could drink until drinking nearly killed me. I found myself twisted. Living to hide. And that ugly half of me kept saying, "You're not good enough. You'll never amount to anything. You blew your chance. You got skipped for the promotion. You're an ugly, downright useless waste. Keep drinking."

I thought I was hiding it well. Until one day, I drove for three and half hours to a safe place because I had this sickness come over me.

I thought that it would be better off if I killed myself.

I'm going to stop here and tell you that there were many times that my mom and loved ones tried to convince me to get help. I, knowing better, didn't listen until something forced me to.

We all have ways we deal with baggage. Not the baggage you excitedly wait for by the carousel at the airport. It's the stack of ugly, unclaimed baggage that gets buried or lost in transit. It's bumped, bruised, scuffed up and looks like it ought to be thrown away. I was asking myself to unpack stuff I had tucked away so privately that I think part of me tried to forget it ever happened. During this personal unveiling ceremony, I felt so, so terrified.

I had insisted on carrying this crap around for 30 years. It was really ugly. It made little sense.

But I did it. I did it because I couldn't bear the pain and anguish my life was causing my mom. So, I opened up and told her how as a child family members through 16 years had sexually assaulted and abused me.

I explained it was not only one family member. I had seen some pretty grotesque things, and I didn't know how to be physically touched or secure around people I wanted love from. I unboxed things like not understanding love ,because my definition of love had gotten messed up at four years old, or as early as I have memories. I approached the individuals who had hurt me and forgave them so that I could move on.

I started wanting to live again.

The world became much more colorful and fun without all the baggage. I rediscovered my faith and accepted God as my father and friend. I fell in love with a great guy who accepted me unconditionally (maybe he likes fixer-uppers). We married, joined houses and had three kids. I started coaching swimming.

I started exercising and coaching people on healthy living principles and nutrition. I volunteered for several nonprofits in my community and mentored young people. I started a new business where I can release my creativity, analytical, and nerdiness.

I discovered that many leaders are high achievers. We are individuals who cannot sit still, and we thrive off a little chaos and control. We may all have stories, but when leaders fall down, they have the air pressure to bounce back up. Often, these bounces lead to shifts in our lifestyle, circle of influence, or career paths.

Leaders find solutions to problems for themselves and others. Often, we thrive from having the best outcome for all parties involved. When leaders discover they aren't on the right track, they shift plans or strategies to align with their goals. Leaders set unrealistic goals, expectations, and standards, which is why it is critically important to have trusted advisors and friends to help ground us. And when something doesn't feel right, a leader knows to ask for help.

Good leadership isn't just about leading others; it's also leading ourselves to know we're not alone to make all decisions. We always require good leadership to have success.

When you know who you are, you get results

By Gina Lokken

Minneapolis, Minnesota

Leadership is typically depicted as position, power or status, and although this may be true, it is only a half-truth. If you ask me, it only represents one side of the coin, the dirtier side. In Old English, the root word for leadership is loedan, which means "to guide, to bring forth." To guide is to look after, guard, accompany, or show the way. Bring forth is to rear, nurture, produce, or give rise to. This definition shows that leadership is more about cultivation and growth than position and power.

Over the years, I've worked for many managers and bosses, but sadly, no leaders; no one I would choose to follow or walk into the proverbial fire with. The problem is that many people placed in positions of power are ill-equipped, not necessarily because they cannot lead, but because they weren't given the proper opportunity to cultivate and grow themselves as a leader. And if you can't lead (guide and bring forth) yourself, you can't lead (guide and bring forth) someone else. To cultivate and nurture the leader within, you first have to recognize and celebrate who you are, what you were designed to do, and who you're equipped to serve. Only then can you help nurture, guide, and influence those around you.

Identity: Who are you?

To become a great leader requires a good deal of self-awareness and self-management. It requires knowing who you are, and what you believe in and value. Without a strong sense of self, there is no internal stability. This lack of self-awareness results in what I call Dr. Jekyll and Mr. Hyde Syndrome; a phenomenon in which a leader flip-flops between strong, juxtaposing emotions when times get hard, thus leading to instability in their relationships. Without a deep understanding of your usual way of being (mindset, behaviors, habits, blind spots, strengths and weaknesses), it's near impossible to cultivate positive influence. This is partially because everyone in your circle of influence fixates on which version of you (good, bad or ugly) they're going to get that day.

Leadership expert John C. Maxwell coined the saying, "Leadership is influence, nothing more, nothing less." Leadership is not about power, not about position; it's about influence. And you're influencing people all the time (spouses, kids, office peers, clerks at the grocery store etc.) for the good and the bad. Meaning your influence is adding value to someone's life or subtracting value. When you know who you are and act on it, you create stability, consistency and trust with those around you.

Design: In what do you excel?

Great leaders not only know who they are but also cultivate the God-given talents in themselves and others. Before Dr. Donald Clifton, the founder and father of strengths-based psychology, died in 2003, he was asked what was the most significant takeaway in his 30 years of research on human potential? He replied:

"A leader needs to know his strengths as a carpenter knows his tools, or as a physician knows the instruments at her disposal. What great leaders have in common is that each knows his or her strengths—and can call on the right strength at the right time. This explains why there is no definitive list of characteristics that describes all leaders."

How well do you understand, articulate, and cultivate your strengths? The raw potential you were given before you were born? The things you naturally excel at? It's hard to put these unique talents into words because they come naturally; it's difficult to imagine that everyone can't do them. And there's the catch. You will have relational friction when you believe everyone should do, think, or work the same way as you. What great leaders practice is what Dr. Clifton found in his research, writing, "They truly know their strengths—and can call on the right strength at the right time." And I would add, they know how to call out the right strengths at the right time in those they lead. You can cultivate engagement and lasting impact when you know who you are and what you excel in. Plus, when you know what you aren't good at, you can find others on your team to fill the gap.

Impact: Where is your greatest opportunity to serve others?

One hallmark of a great leader is that they're able to maximize their contribution to the communities they're best positioned to serve. They place themselves where their unique style, passions, gifts and talents have the best opportunity to positively affect the lives of those around them—they not only have a positive influence but a wide one. This kind of lasting ripple effect on individuals and communities is produced by seeing and acting on the needs (emotional, physical, circumstantial, etc.) which nurtures and grows the potential of others while concurrently increasing the leader's influence exponentially.

So, what are you aiming for? Results or relationships? Great leaders are less "me" focused and more "we" focused, less selfish and more selfless. If done properly and with the right motives, this type of leadership produces faster, effortless results. When you know and address the needs of the community or organization you are best equipped to serve, you build an unshakable culture of belonging and the results will far outweigh what you ever thought possible.

When you know who you are, you get results

If leadership is more about cultivation and growth than position and power, then leaders with an acute awareness of who they are, their God-given talents, and the needs of those around them, are the best equipped to help nurture and grow those in their sphere of influence. This kind of leadership brings forth more healthy leaders, something our society and culture desperately need, because when you know who you are, you get results.

I leave you with this question? What have you done to cultivate yourself into someone who lives and leads with excellence?

You, then them; them, then you

By Dr. Whitnie Wiley

Elk Grove, California

We are all leaders. Not all of us run companies or have fancy titles, but in our lives, we are leaders.

Whether you are leading yourself, your family, your community, your country, or the world you are a leader.

When you come to understand that leadership is not about you but about those you lead, that's when you have the makings of being a great leader. The question is how? How do you become great at leading regardless of who you lead? Recognizing it starts with you, but it does not end there.

But before you can focus on becoming a great leader, you must decide what you want. You must determine what kind of leader you want to be; an accidental one or an exceptional one? If exceptional, continue reading.

Leadership is not about you, yet it's all about you.

It's about you understanding who you are and how you impact others.

It's about you choosing to uplift and empower others so that they can be the best they can be.

It's about you learning how to serve and give so that others will choose to do the same.

It's about you knowing why you are leading and fully committing to that why.

It's about you sharing your time, talents and treasures, and everything that is at your disposal and then influencing others to do the same.

It's about you bringing the fullness of yourself, shifting the energy in every room so that others are enthusiastic about moving collectively toward a shared vision.

In a word, it's SIMPLE.

SIMPLE is an acronym that stands for Self-awareness, Intentionality, Mastery, Purposefulness, Leverage, and Energy.

When you incorporate these elements into your personal development, you become a better person. When you're better, you lead better.

That's when the magic happens, and you become the leader that even you would follow.

I've always been a rebel, determined to do things my way, and to my detriment. Despite constantly being placed in leadership positions, I hadn't always seen myself as a leader. Truth be told, I had given little thought to what being a leader meant.

As I progressed through school, then later at work, I saw the benefits of being the leader—or what I thought a leader was; being in charge. Being top dog allowed me to do things my way. While I wasn't abusive with my power, I didn't focus on the need to bring along those serving alongside me either.

I was about getting it done. Taking the time to find out how to use others better to reach a goal wasn't something I'd given thought to. Interestingly, you don't know what hot is until you have something to compare. And I didn't know what it was to work for bad leaders until I worked for some excellent ones.

As mentioned, I didn't give leadership or whether I was good at it much thought, until it mattered. It mattered because it impacted my ability to deliver the depth and breadth of what I could provide in my work, and for the constituency I served. So, I paid attention. As I observed what was happening around me, I noted what those in leadership positions did and didn't do well, and how it impacted others.

Did they lift people or tear them down? Did they pick up the energy in the room or drain it? Were they being honest or leaving their integrity at the door? Did they notice or care what those they led needed?

I reflected on my various stints of being in similar positions. I had done none of those things. I wasn't focused on anything other than how I looked and whether it would allow me to move to the next level? It was a problematic mirror to stare into, and I didn't like what I saw.

By this time, I'd had a couple of challenging situations in my life that broke me open. These experiences helped me understand my need to approach life and relationships differently. It was not only that I'd matured, but also that I was willing to view my life's experiences as opportunities to learn and grow.

I mention relationships because one thing I learned on my journey is that outstanding leadership is about relationships.

It's not about your title or wielding power. It's about how you relate to and interact with others, and how you can influence them to work with you to reach your shared vision or objective.

It doesn't matter if it's creating the next big thing, manufacturing smartphones, or serving meals at the local shelter. Do people choose to follow you when they have a choice? And once they have, do you leave them better than when you first met them?

In the end it boils down to this. You get to be whatever kind of leader you choose to be. The problem with many leaders is they fail to create a vision for themselves or their team.

They spend little time or energy thinking of their actual role or what they want to accomplish, and how they will empower those they lead to get it done. If that's your approach, you're leaving your potential to be excellent on the table. Switch your focus to your team by clarifying your purpose and putting team member needs above yours.

Decide from the outset what kind of leader you want to be, and who you need to be as a person to be that kind of leader. To be a better leader, be a better person. It's SIMPLE.

Overcoming adversity

By Sheba Wilson

Turks and Caicos Islands

There is a common trait in each person who has achieved greatness—their response in the face of adversity. Life is challenging; we all face circumstances in our lives that are unexpected and painful. We do not control what we will encounter in life, but we have complete control over our response to those circumstances. As the late Carnegie Mellon Professor Randy Pausch so eloquently put it, "We cannot change the hand we are dealt, just how we play the game."

What do you do with the space between stimuli and response? How do you handle adversity? What makes one person choose to accept defeat and another, taking the challenge to overcome adversity? It is a matter of mindset, that internal monologue that scores every aspect of our lives. Our collection of thoughts and beliefs shapes our thought habits and affects how we think, what we feel, and how we respond. It impacts how we view ourselves and the world.

In her book, *Mindset: The New Psychology of Success*, Carol Dweck explains the difference between a fixed and a growth mindset. Those with a fixed mindset avoid challenges, whereas persons with a growth mindset persevere in the face of adversity. Growth minded individuals see opportunities in hardships and keep pushing forward, while others give up easily and believe their efforts are fruitless and their abilities are limited.

I am all too familiar with adversity and loss. In 2015, I unexpectedly lost my best friend of over 25 years; two months later, I lost my husband to stage 4 prostate cancer. We had an 18 month battle, and I was prayerful and hopeful that he would beat cancer. Upon receiving the diagnosis, I immediately sprung into solution mode. I researched diet and holistic medicine versus chemotherapy. I juggled caring for my spouse while working full time, raising our children and serving as chairperson on a government board.

There were days I was physically tired and emotionally drained. In those times, the only source of strength I had to keep me going was an unexplainable faith in God, and a mindset that we had to fight and win. Even when my husband lost hope, I was still expecting a miracle.

People told me how strong I was many times, but I didn't feel strong; I felt weak, inadequate.

I didn't realize it, but I was being prepared to be a widow. I was becoming self-sufficient to the natural eye.

A growth mindset coupled with purpose and grit allows people to overcome adversity. Even when you lose, you learn, grow, and prepare for the next phase of the journey.

You may think to yourself, this sounds good, but how do I develop a growth mindset and determine my purpose and act with grit?

1. Find your why. Your "why" is something much greater than the self. German philosopher Friedrich Nietzsche said it this way, "He who has a why to live for can bear almost any how." Psychologists define purpose as, "An abiding intention to achieve a long-term goal that is both personally meaningful and makes a positive mark on the world." If you are unsure about your purpose, focus on the fact that it is not only intellectual. Think back on hurts you have experienced and how you can use them to help others heal. Each of us has a hurt to heal. Find the hurt you are meant to heal in this world, and you'll discover your purpose.

2.   Acknowledge your strengths and weaknesses. Don't become burdened by your weaknesses and don't pretend that you have none. Instead, leverage your strengths and carve out a plan to improve. As you work on those weak areas, you will stretch and grow. While you may never master them, you certainly will develop greater competency.

3.   Be solution-oriented. Growth minded individuals recognize that life will always present challenges, and they are determined to find solutions to those problems. They will try. Even if they don't win, they will learn, regroup and try another way until they are successful.

4.   Be intentional about your self-talk and thoughts. Guard your heart and be mindful of the words you tell yourself. Be intentional about saying only positive, affirmative words of hope to yourself. When negative thoughts enter your mind, always counter them with more positive, hopeful, and motivational ones. The conversations you have with yourself are the most important words you will ever hear. If you believe you can do something, you will, and if you believe you can't, you won't. Believe that you can overcome whatever challenges you have to face.

5.   Accept criticism as a gift. When you receive feedback, be open-minded. Others may see your actions from a perspective you may not have considered. Sometimes the suggestions offered are valuable and beneficial to you in overcoming challenges and improving processes and outcomes.

6.   Be brave. Adverse circumstances can feel debilitating and cause you to feel stuck. It doesn't have to be that way; you have the power to reframe challenging circumstances in your mind and see them as opportunities for a new adventure, one in which you can learn, grow and triumph. Fear is a valid feeling, but you must prepare to push beyond your fears and discover what lies ahead.

7.   Strive for progress, not perfection. Perfection is a fantasy; it is not attainable. Instead of perfection, strive to make progress each day. We all have flaws and inefficiencies. Likewise, we have great strengths; use your strengths as much as possible. Focus on the discoveries, enjoy the journey and celebrate your small wins.

If you desire to overcome adverse circumstances and build resilience, start embracing challenges as opportunities and commit to persisting in the face of adversity. You must also prepare to take control of responsibility for your thoughts, words, and actions. Overcoming adversity requires that you acknowledge that your effort will determine your level of mastery and resilience.

Leadership

Authentic leadership

By Larry Levine

Featured author
Los Angeles, California

"It's hard to practice compassion when we're struggling with our authenticity or when our own worthiness is off-balance." - Brene Brown.

Authenticity is one of the biggest challenges in the world of leadership. Often, it's a challenge for a leader to be themselves and show strength. Leaders should embrace authenticity. Leaders who are comfortable in their skin can focus on leading and not having to create a mask of "be all" and "know it all."

What is authenticity? It's staying true to who you are, what you do, whom you serve and why you do what you do.

To quote Simon Sinek: "It means that the things we say and the things we do are things we actually believe."

It sounds touchy-feely but look inside yourself. Leadership is all about building credible, genuine relationships. To build these relationships and change the way people think, you need to understand who you are and what goods you bring to the table. Here lies the issue for many appointed leaders—they fail because they have not invested in themselves.

> *"Authenticity is the daily practice of letting go of who we think we are supposed to be and embracing who we actually are."* - Brené Brown.

Authenticity requires self-knowledge and self-awareness. Authentic leaders accept their strengths and weaknesses. They are accountable to themselves. They connect to their values and desires and act deliberately consistent with those qualities.

Are you an authentic leader?

Authentic leaders are genuine, caring, and nurturing. Authentic leaders build relationships and build true connectedness with their team. They will share their deepest personal experiences and listen to the experiences of others.

Authentic leaders have a heart, which shows in their compassion for others. They are sensitive to the needs of others and will help each team member.

Leaders who lead and serve from the heart develop teams that serve from the heart

Authentic leaders rise and lead with courage, compassion, and conviction in times of uncertainty, concern, fear, and transformational situations.

Authentic leaders are consistent with their message. They are focused and determined to positively impact each member of their team.

Create a self-aware team

A self-aware team means they know themselves and they become amazingly happy, which allows them to live an enriched and balanced life.

I encourage you to think about the following questions:

• Is each member on your team the real deal, or are they trying to be someone else? Would you even know?

• Do their thoughts match their actions? Would you even know?

• Does their walk match their talk? Would you even know?

When you and your team live outside of the truth, it comes out eventually. It will negatively impact your team, your relationships, and your team's relationships with clients.

Create a team that self-reflects

What makes you tick? What makes each member of your team tick?

Knowing yourself brings you face-to-face with self-doubts and insecurities. Self-reflecting allows you to take a serious look at how you are living your life.

A vulnerable leader is not weak. A vulnerable leader is strong, sensitive, and supportive.

Getting to know yourself is a conscious effort. Authentic leaders lead with intent and purpose.

Are you leading your team with intent, purpose, and pride?

Authenticity is a choice. It is difficult, but this is the difference between merely getting by and making it happen. Self-reflect for a moment, asking yourself what it means to lead an authentic lifestyle? It is hard work. It is looking right into the mirror, asking tough questions and answering them.

What is your plan for your team? What do you need to do with your team right now? It is totally up to you! Open up who you are to your team and watch them become authentic leaders.

Authentic leaders rise and are not afraid to draw a line in the sand and ask,

"Are you with me?"

The dangers of being inauthentic

You must realize, your team members are smarter and more empowered than ever before. They can see through your mask, the charades and all "about me" attitudes. Especially in turbulent times, the teams that embrace authenticity and stay true to themselves will be successful in today's digitally dominated world.

I'd asked you to think about the following:

- What would happen if every member on my team brought the real, raw and relatable version of themselves to the business table?

- What would happen if every team member opened the window into who they are?

Authentic leaders double down on their team

In a chaotic and crisis-filled world, leaders invest.

- Are you doubling down on your team and yourself?

- Are you doubling down with your customers?

In uncertain times, leaders rise and double down on re-inventing, re-engaging, re-educating, re-igniting and re-committing to their teams.

Ignite your mind, your heart and your sense of community.

> *"Leaders who don't listen will eventually be surrounded by people who have nothing to say." -*
> Andy Stanley.

Endurance leadership: The guts for greatness in a world of quick wins

By Ann Bowers-Evangelista
Washington. D.C.

Endurance leadership is a novel concept that helps leaders move past the short-term, constant sprint mentality that can lead to stress, burnout, and anxiety. Leveraging the strategies and tactics used by endurance athletes, leaders can build a lifetime of leadership success.

Endurance Leadership Model

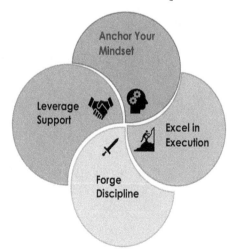

Anchor your mindset

1. Know your Mission. Sometimes understood as your "why" you can identify your Mission by asking, "What am I uniquely on the planet to do?" or "What do I want people/my family to say about me at the end of my life?" These deep and powerful questions help leaders tap into the intrinsic motivators that keep them going when things get tough.

2. Know your baseline. Endurance athletes take stock of their current fitness levels before planning a strategy to achieve a race goal. Are you doing the same? Have you sought data to determine how close you are to achieving your leadership development goals? Feedback from stakeholders, targeted assessments, or coach observations all help you understand where you are relative to your goal, so you can set a reasonable and explicit plan.

3. Build the plan. Like someone planning to run the Boston Marathon, once you know what you want to achieve and how close you are to achieving it, set specific plans to get there. A mission is a lifetime journey, but you can break your plan for success into short and long-term chunks. Look high-level at five year goals, but build specificity into the one year, six month, and monthly plans.

4. Prepare for obstacles. There will be obstacles to achieving your plan. You may be planning to expand your family or take a big vacation. Plan for those moments, so they don't throw you off your game when they occur.

Excel in execution

1. Train every day. Endurance athletes train every day, even if it's rest or something outside of their sport. What minimum viable effort can you make to improve against your leadership goal? Commit to small units of execution to keep you focused and energized around goal achievement.

2. Use the Action-Reflection Cycle. Without conscious reflection, endurance athletes and leaders can continue to make costly mistakes. Finding time for regular reflection (even if only for a moment) can give your efforts clarity and direction.

3.   Run the mile you are in. Taken from marathons, this means that when challenges arise on the long road to success, focus on what you can control. Thoughts and actions that help you maintain self-efficacy, fuel optimism, and forward momentum.Learn to pace. An athlete trying to sprint a marathon will fatigue early and risk injury. The same is true for leaders. Plan for the moments when you need to sprint at work, but set clear rules regarding when the sprinting will cease. Being intentional about pace can help you (and your team) maintain energy and focus, keeping you in the long game.

4.   Recover. Recovery is critical for athlete success; why would it be different for leader success? Commit time for recovery: Adequate sleep, exercise, meditation, small breaks, and family time are all strategies. Determine what approach works best for you, but do not leave it to chance—plan for recovery every day.

Forge discipline

1.   Build mental toughness. While resilience can help you bounce back from adversity, mental toughness helps endurance leaders thrive in the face of future challenges. Build mental toughness by pushing outside your comfort zone. Seek out contrasting points of view, challenge conventional thinking, or put yourself in new environments where success is not automatic. These approaches will build your ability and confidence to thrive in less than ideal conditions.

2.   Build agility. Think of this as leadership cross-training; the more varied environments you spend time in, the more adaptable you will be in the face of unforeseen circumstances. Work in another part of the business, find a mentor from a different industry, consult with innovators on your team. Agility makes you stronger and enhances mental toughness.

3.   Embrace the epic fail. Sometimes the best-laid plans still fall short. Recognize these moments and embrace their learning potential. Rather than become frustrated or reactive, ask yourself, "What is creating this situation? What can I learn from it? What path might I pursue instead?" Manage and grow from failure, rather than let it manage you.

Leverage support

1. Get a coach. Like endurance athletes, find a coach fundamentally focused on one thing: Making you better.

2. Make anyone a coach. Leverage key stakeholders, mentors, family members, or friends to provide less formal support and accountability on your growth journey. Creating a network of informal coaches can help you stay focused, accountable, and on track.

3. Fall in love with metrics. Endurance athletes are obsessed with metrics that tell them how they perform and precisely where to target their improvement efforts—track metrics related to your targeted behavioral change every day. Apps and online resources can help you track productivity, goal success, and even physiological states that can help you stay on track with leadership goals. Remember, what gets measured gets done.

4. Build an attitude of gratitude. Substantial research shows gratitude is an essential mediating variable in motivation, self-improvement, and productivity in both endurance athletes and endurance leaders. Introduce appreciation into meetings; keep a gratitude journal and share gratitude at home or through service to others. It will help you maintain perspective and keep your long-term vision.

The future of successful leadership will require strategies that extend far beyond short-term, "quick-win" approaches. By adopting an endurance leadership approach, leaders can cultivate greatness for decades.

The leader in you

By Ulunda N. Baker

Charlotte, North Carolina

I got on my bike and rode up to the local McDonald's. I ordered happy meals for each one of them. I took my $33.00 paycheck I worked so hard for and spent it on food that evening because we had none. I rode my bike back to my house, and as I stood in front of the kitchen table watching my siblings eat their food, smiling and laughing with each other, it sealed my sadness.

This was the first moment in my life when I realized there was a leader in me.

It wasn't the first time I took money from my part-time job and shared it with my siblings or others in need. I made a conscious choice to put them or others before myself at an early age. Being the oldest of seven siblings and living in an unstable home situation, I felt the pull to step up and lead. My goal in life was to free myself from the web of generational struggles, including poverty, drugs, abuse, homelessness, and mental health struggles, no matter what it took.

When I look back on my life story and where I am now, I see where the adversities directly shaped me as a leader. I am a first-generation corporate

America leader in my family with 10 plus years of experience leading people, processes, organizational growth and change. Despite how strong I feel as a leader, there are times when I still feel unqualified. Who am I to lead? I don't have an MBA or any certifications. But I have my experiences, bumps, bruises, and scars of battle from my life.

My son recently did a school essay on what it takes to be a good leader. He asked me to share my important aspects of leading. I narrowed down my top two.

Leadership takes sacrifice

Vince Lombardi said, "Leaders are made, they are not born. They are made by hard effort, which is the price which all of us must pay to achieve any goal that is worthwhile."

My goal as a child was to overcome and lead my family. My goal professionally is to lead just as well; for example, like growing up and having to put my siblings and family first. I make that decision at home, at work, and as a leader in my community every day. I willingly give my natural gifts, time, experience, finances, and an extreme amount of personal energy.

Leadership is hard, and it comes with the payment of sacrifice. At least three times in my career, I intentionally elevated people on my team, even if it meant no promotion or a raise for me. If you choose to step into a leadership capacity, know that you may give away or lose something for yourself; but the space created from your sacrifice will refill with the repayment of growth and achievement of your goal, which is to be a good leader.

Take care of you

During my childhood struggles, I learned how to sacrifice too well, sometimes to the detriment of myself. I carried the heavy burden of caring for my siblings and myself way more than I should've had to. It was emotionally, physically, and mentally taxing for me as a child, teenager, and even into adulthood. As a leader at work and in the community, I've felt that same taxing. Eventually, I had no choice but to seek therapy, coaching, and other resources to help me unpack years of trauma and learn how to be a strong and healthy leader.

I try to be conscious of how I felt about facing leadership roles. Being a leader doesn't make you immune to being human, and it doesn't keep you from breaking. I believe it's our responsibility as leaders to take ownership of taking care of ourselves. When the pressure of leadership gets too much, I commit to myself to follow a key set of affirmations. Do not be afraid to express:

- I need help. Asking doesn't make me a weak leader. It means I am human.
- I am taking a day for myself.
- I am getting some coaching and training so that I can be better.
- I am seeking the advice of my therapist, doctor or sphere of support.
- I need to secure myself before I can help you.
- I am stepping back until I can take on more.
- I am my best advocate.

I created this list eight years ago after I resigned from a job at the peak of my corporate career. I was climbing the corporate ladder and succeeding. I had a great salary, traveled, and had an exceptional growth plan as a leader. But the weight from relocating, workload and personal struggles at home became too much for me. I struggled to bring my best and whole self to work. I failed my team. I stepped back with grace and resigned.

Looking back on that moment and all the moments, good or bad, in my life, I have no regrets. I have my health, family, career, community, and a whole and healthy Ulunda.

Marry the vision, date the strategy

By Jason Cutter
Fort Myers, Florida

The leadership quote I live by is, "Marry the vision, date the strategy." I cannot remember where or when I heard it, but let me explain why it's so valuable and how it helps to succeed at leading. The challenge is that the primal part of our brains (amygdala) likes safety, security, and the known, and prefers to stay within our comfort zone. We avoid change and must feel SAFE: *Successful At Fear Elimination*, before we move forward. By definition, as a leader, you are leading a group of people or an organization to somewhere unfamiliar. It is also important to understand that your leadership goal is pulling people along on the path with you. You want followers to be part of the journey compared to managing (the person, task, project), which is about pushing it to completion across the finish line. People do not enjoy micromanaging, the ultimate form of pushing with the smallest increments possible.

There are three keys to success as a leader for pulling followers.

First, you must know where you want to go. Rarely will people blindly follow someone without an actual destination or goal in mind. Sure, there are always people who will jump in the car with you and get on the road and "see where we end up," but it takes having a WHY for that to happen. You must have a clearly stated vision.

A second key for leadership is having the WHY—the mission; the reason the leader is doing what they are doing, and why they are recruiting followers. The promise of a fun, memorable road trip could prove to be a big enough WHY, but the where doesn't matter. The bigger the mission, the more people will commit to the vision.

Third, effective leadership requires understanding what others want and need, and how the mission, vision, and core values of the leader/organization fit into the goals of those individuals. Many leaders fall in love with their vision and they assume everyone will want to be on board with the mission. And yes, sometimes that works out, or if you are a certain kind of leader you play the numbers game, by talking to enough people to find the ones who resonate with where you are going.

When you learn more about the other person; what they want, their hopes and dreams, their fears and experiences, you can determine if what you are offering as a leader and where you are going fits their potential path. This is an important part of being an amazing leader—knowing who is on board with you and then treating them as individuals.

It is critical to leadership success because humans in general view themselves as the center of their universe—the hero of their story and life. We all do. That is part of human existence. Yes, we are a tribal society, but we care about ourselves and our needs, wants, and survival at our core.

The people you are leading feel that same way, deep down inside. It will have a limited effect when leaders make it all about themselves and what they want to accomplish. And that strategy is reliant on charisma, excitement, and hoping followers want the same thing. When leaders understand the individuals on their team and know what they want, they can help them to buy-in.

One last suggestion to help your leadership effectiveness is to always account for change. When I am hiring for any position, I set the expectation that change is a constant. Things will not always go as planned. Unwanted situations will occur. Pivoting will be necessary. You cannot predict or control where life will lead you and your team. The best thing you can do is prepare the people you lead for change before it occurs.

This leads me back to my leadership quote, "Marry the vision, date the strategy" and why it is vital for effectively leading your team, individual, or organization. People, because of their desire to avoid change and to stay in their known comfort zone, want to marry the vision and the strategy. The challenge is that the strategy will need to change. Sometimes constantly. Sometimes in big ways.

As a leader, your priority is to ensure that everyone marries into the vision—where you are taking them. That destination is locked in. How you get there, what it looks like, what technology you use, what road you take, etc., is the strategy, and you want your team dating the strategy—if they trust you, they will follow it every day. Build a vision that people can marry. Share the mission and why that vision is important to you and for each person. Then help your followers embrace the act of dating as many strategies as it takes to achieve the vision.

When done properly, the mindset of a sales professional is as a leader to their prospective clients. Reread the above and replace "follower" and "people" with "prospect," and you will also have the formula for persuading and selling at a high level.

High-Performance Leadership Trifecta

By Gary P. Kooper, Kooper Leadership Academy
Florence, South Carolina

Have you wondered why some people always seem to be focused? No matter how much they have going on, they consistently deliver on their commitments and appear superhuman?

Have you ever thought about what differentiates the common from the uncommon, the leader from the follower, and what can take you to the next level of performance?

The recipe is quite simple, and I call it the High-Performance Leadership Trifecta. It has three primary ingredients:

1. Time - The great equalizer

2. Focus - Do simple better

3. Effort - The power is in you

When combined with a clear purpose and the unwavering commitment to excel, each of these primary ingredients will help you get to your next level of performance.

Time

There are 86,400 seconds in a day, and we all have the same 24 hours. That is why I refer to the first ingredient, time, as the great equalizer. The great equalizer has a way of settling the score and punishing those who spend time in distracted and non-value work. It is choices like these that will put you behind in your work, create more stress, and place you where your work product does not reflect your best.

However, in these same 24 hours, the high-performing leader intentionally optimizes their time, undistracted and with the single-mindedness of meeting their commitments. There are no excuses for the high performer; time is a resource that must be valued and protected at all costs.

Quote to ponder: "It's easy to get undisciplined with the choices we make, and it's with these choices we remember that time waits for no one."

Action to consider: Look at your last 24 hours and write about those things that kept you from delivering on your commitments. Can you identify the non-value avoidance activity?

Focus

We live in a world of distractions, a world where instant gratification feeds the desire for constant affirmation (do you know how many likes you got on your recent post?). We live in a world where the dinging of your device triggers a conditioned response (think Pavlov's Dogs theory), where we feel the need to consume in large bites (consider binge-watching an entire season of your favorite show). It is easy to see how society has become incapable of focusing on how we live. By understanding the importance of three words, Do Simple Better, high performers can get to the core of the next Trifecta ingredient, Focus, and separate themselves from the rest.

Doing simple better means separating the distractions and background noise, and honing in on those key areas that have the biggest impact on achieving your daily goals and actions. Focus like this requires discipline, routine, and being comfortable with the word "NO." It doesn't mean you don't engage in active listening to ensure alignment, but it does mean you don't waiver in meeting your commitments.

Doing simple better means focusing on the critical few areas that will ensure understanding, action, and measurable results.

Quote to ponder: "Discipline isn't something you are born with. It's a daily choice you make."

Action to consider: Look at your current list of things to do and distill these down to the absolute critical few: Simplify + Focus + Execution = High-Performance Results.

Effort

The third ingredient to high-performance leadership is effort. Effort involves understanding and embracing that the power is in you. We live in a society where blaming others for the barriers we face, whether real or perceived, is easy. The reward goes to those who show up, not those who rise above and deliver. Finally, testing yourself every day is perceived as being over the top, insensitive, or simply aggressive.

High-performance leadership requires uncommon effort to achieve uncommon results. It requires leaders to identify the goal they want to achieve, and then commit unwaveringly to a routine of daily habits and actions that focus on goal achievement.

Effort requires leaders to move beyond their comfort zone and the mental self-talk that tells you to, "slow down" to "stop" or "you can do this tomorrow."

We require effort to overcome the mental barrier of "self-protection" and reset our mental muscle.

Life will test your commitment. You must be prepared to earn it; no hacks, no shortcuts. A simply extraordinary effort will take you to the next level of high-performance leadership.

Quote to ponder: "You are your biggest enemy, and to win in life, you must overcome the weakness that lies between your ears."

Action to consider: Think about one goal in your personal, professional, and community life. What activities are you performing to achieve that goal, and what are your current results? What if you could put in 15 more minutes of intentional effort, one more repetition, one more call, and one more act of gratitude every day for 30, 60, or 90 days?

Kooper's Korner

With 27 years of marriage, four children, a 30 year career in operations, leadership coaching, mentoring, and my journey toward high-performance, I have found the areas of time management, Focus, and Effort to be key ingredients to continued high-performance growth.

Make no doubt about it, the journey will be difficult. It will test your resolve, and it will break you to your core. It's in these times that you are building the mental strength to achieve greatness.

High-performance leadership begins with waking up each day, looking in the mirror, and saying, "It's up to me, and I can make a difference."

Take a moment to breathe

By Kate Lake
Lakeland, Florida

L eadership is the compilation of many qualities managed together to create desired outcomes. Excellent leadership begins with a response-based mindset.

A friend once found himself in a strange, frightening predicament that could have proven deadly if he had not started with the right mindset.

For many years, Cesar supported his children's agricultural education and personal development by helping them raise cows. They would care for and feed a calf over nine months until they took it to the state fair.

To store and protect a large amount of feed, they used a small, concrete room with one entrance. It was a solidly constructed, windowless room with a single light bulb hanging in the center of the ceiling. When the light was off and the door shut, the room became pitch black.

Unfortunately, it didn't take long for the local rat population to figure out that the light fixture provided a highway to a terrific food source! They followed the electrical conduit to find the small opening in the ceiling and crawl down into the room whenever it was dark. As a result, it wasn't unusual to see rats scramble out of the room when the light was turned on. Therefore, whenever the family entered the room, they prepared to eliminate the uninvited guests.

One day, Cesar was working in the room when a horse invited himself in for a bite to eat. Before Cesar could get to the horse, the horse's tail closed the door simultaneously as its head bumped the light bulb, causing it to explode. The room suddenly became pitch black.

Cesar faced a serious dilemma. If the horse got spooked, it would thrash out in fear. Besides potentially hurting itself, the horse's kick could severely injure or even kill Cesar in an instant. Therefore, Cesar's priority was to keep the horse calm. He immediately realized that he had to avoid feeling an understandable panic because the horse would sense his emotions.

So Cesar took a moment to breathe and calm his thoughts while quickly assessing the situation. He could hear the horse snorting heavily, shifting its weight from side to side, and preparing to take action. Before long, Cesar's eyes adapted to the pitch-blackness, and he made out the horse's large frame in the middle of the room, blocking his path to the door.

Soon a plan was clear in Cesar's mind. Cesar worked his way around the perimeter of the room, hugging the wall while keeping his thoughts in check. As the minutes ticked by, that dragged as if they were hours, he tried not to wonder whether the rat population would soon join the party.

Happily, Cesar found his way to the door without incident and gave the delighted horse a path to lighted freedom. When Cesar told me this story, I realized he managed an incredibly challenging situation with great skill. He used a repeatable, two-step approach that can help any of us successfully navigate unexpected crises.

First, breathe

When a crisis appears, our adrenaline kicks in. We are ready to react immediately. Alternatively, we can slow our breathing while simultaneously assessing the situation. This method will enable us to respond with a controlled, intentional approach.

The technique for slowing your breathing is simple: Inhale through your nose for four seconds, hold your breath for four seconds, then exhale through your mouth for four seconds. As you do this over and over, your heartbeat will slow down. You will induce a state of calmness within your body.

This approach will work in a variety of circumstances. For example, think back to when you first learned of the COVID crisis in 2020. No one could tell us about how the virus was transmitted. All we knew was that it was spreading fast and causing severe illness, and sometimes death. We all played a game of Simon Says in the first month as we stopped our daily activities and stood still. The crisis affected both business owners and employees. Everyone wondered how they would survive without income.

When answers are not immediately available, stop! Take a moment to breathe.

Next, let your eyes adjust

When the lights go out in a fully enclosed room, it's clear that one must give a moment to let our eyes adjust. However, when we face critical situations in the light of day, our eyes appear to see everything around us. Visual data tricks our minds into incorrectly thinking that we see clearly.

The next time you face a crisis, as you are steadying your breathing, take a moment to let your eyes adjust. When situations arise, it can take a few moments to identify all the changes and determine how they affect you and your goals. At first, it may look like the worst of all circumstances is confronting you. Difficult situations also bring opportunities. Let your eyes adjust and soak in all the details of the challenge facing you. Ask yourself, "Where is the hidden opportunity?" Those who learn to find hidden opportunities in predicaments are the ones who emerge quickly and successfully.

It's about mindset

Leadership starts with learning how to lead ourselves before we lead others. Learn to respond intentionally to difficult circumstances (vs. immediately reacting) by starting with the right mindset. This method is how you will achieve your desired outcome more quickly.

Leading the 4 life stages of teams

By Mark McCatty, Leadership and Team Advisor
Tampa, Florida

A team is a collection of people who combine their talents to accomplish a shared goal. We've all seen teams with tremendous individual skills yet cannot get it across the goal line. Not all teams are successful. The difference between successful and ineffective teams is their ability to go through the stages quickly. And it's easier to get things moving when some momentum is generated. Successful teams have a deep understanding of personal and collective strengths, and each team member cooperates with the other members to reach their shared objectives and honor their shared values.

The leadership golden nugget? After working with leaders and teams for over 20 years, I've developed my leadership philosophy. "In the absence of commitment, all you have is half-hearted compliance or whole-hearted defiance."

That's it! In teams or any other relationship, if you don't have a commitment from those involved, then you have a lackluster effort or downright obstinance. With teams, leaders need to work hard to develop commitment.

The 4 stages of successful teams

A team is a group of people who work toward a common goal while demonstrating respect for each other. Respect is a key characteristic of uncommon teams. Respect is observable. Team behaviors are present and easy to see and easy to assess. It is also possible to assess the quality of the leadership behaviors shown by the team's membership.

The 4 stages of a team:

1. Foundation
2. Business Focus
3. Release Power
4. Sustain

Stage 1 - Foundation: At this level, the team forms and explores the experiences of being a team. Teaming requires different skill sets; it needs social awareness and more highly tuned people skills. Initially, a group holds together by a bonding of similarity. When people align around what is similar, positive things can happen. Bonding is critical to people. We want to be part of the tribe, and we find others we are attracted to. The challenge is that this creates cliques that are non-productive for effective teaming. Teams must move beyond adhesion; being attracted to similarities, to cohesion; maintaining attraction to dissimilarities. Leaders create the climate for teams to succeed by providing direction and support for the team process. Often, additional team training skills beyond the technical skills required for completing the task are required.

In this foundation stage of teams, participants learn what it is like to work effectively with others. They think and act like a team, and provide more support to each other. They are intentional about demonstrating respect for the other team members. But their focus can become more myopic about the team and not the mission.

Stage 2 - Business Focus: At this level, the team understands and takes on the purpose for their team. Newly formed teams can be excited and motivated by a new opportunity. Now the teams need to turn their motivation toward accomplishing their purpose. Leaders inspire alignment around the common goals and assess the team's understanding of their purpose. As teams focus on accomplishing specific tasks, they become more motivated. Progress continues...

As teams experience greater understanding and ownership for the team's purpose, increased opportunity for ownership becomes available within the team.

Stage 3 - Release Power: At this level, the team becomes more empowered and takes on more responsibility. As teams develop and show signs of accomplishment, management delegates responsibility. Suppose there is no process or development plan to support the team or allow the team to pick up these responsibilities. This delegation is referred to as dumping. So, leadership has a heavy responsibility to create an engaging and supportive climate for the team. Teams are more inclined to take greater control over their work and arrange conditions for their success once they've reached this stage of team development. Release of power planning is a structured process that allows the team to advance through this stage more quickly. By defining future expectations for the team to control, and planning and supporting this transition, teams can successfully navigate through stage 3 and move rapidly to the final stage.

Stage 4 - Sustain: At this level, the team provides more self-direction and sustains their growth through the process of continual improvement. Teams will experience failure; and there is a benefit from failure. Teams, like people, grow through a learning process filled with successes and failures. When teams learn and progress from failure, then team failures are a benefit to the team. Organizationally, other teams can benefit from sharing the lessons learned. The successful lessons discovered from teams at this level are shared, rather than allowing each team to learn its lessons through trial and error.

> *"In the absence of commitment, all you have is half-hearted compliance or whole-hearted defiance."* - Mark McCatty.

Leadership is responsible

Everything rises or falls on leadership. John Maxwell's *15th Law of Teamwork* states that the difference between two equally talented teams is leadership. Leadership makes the difference. Good leaders have developed a high self-awareness. And wise leaders have learned to lead themselves successfully before they attempt to lead others. After all, leading yourself is usually the hardest person you will ever have to lead. You cannot take someone to a place you have never been yourself. You can point them in the right direction; but only someone who has gone down the path can show others the path.

Leadership's responsibilities for each stage:

- Stage 1: Provide structure, direction, and team member skills training.
- Stage 2: Provide training and resources for business management and the associated decisions.
- Stage 3: Provide strategic clarity regarding future team responsibilities and empowerment levels.
- Stage 4: Support a climate conducive to learning and continual improvement.

Team leadership requires moving beyond individual contribution. It means developing commitment in others. It means uniting diverse individuals who think about things differently. Building people with diverse backgrounds and experiences to join around shared values to pursue a common goal. It means generating engagement that will inspire people to make personal sacrifices for the identified team purpose. Stage 4 teams have developed maturity and clarity of purpose and action. Leaders help teams develop clarity of understanding around values, goals, and roles and responsibilities. Without this simple clarity and commitment, teamwork suffers. When teamwork suffers, the team fails.

The importance of true servant leadership

By Marques Ogden

Raleigh Durham, North Carolina

L eadership is not a title. Leadership is not a privilege; it is not a position that should abuse power. True leadership is the responsibility to serve others. It is the responsibility to serve a cause greater than yourself. It is the true aspiration to put everyone's needs and desires above your own. When I think of leaders, I think of people like Martin Luther King Jr., Rosa Parks, Mother Teresa, Gandhi, Nelson Mandela and others. These great leaders were about the cause; they were about serving greater humanity; they were about helping to create a better universe, and for these reasons, they are leaders in my eyes.

In 2008, I started a construction company in Baltimore, Maryland. I ended up reaching a high pinnacle of success with this endeavor. By the beginning of 2012, I was the largest African American owned site work contractor in Baltimore and Maryland. I was on top of the world, I could do no wrong. Everything I said and or did I thought I was always right. This kind of attitude consumed me.

In 2012, I metamorphosed from a good, humble, inclusive leader into an egocentric, loudmouthed, arrogant maniac who was his own worst enemy. I literally had an ego the size of the Empire State Building, and it got to where I literally drove my best employees away, because I did not create a safe and inclusive environment for my trusted team to express themselves. So they went and found other places of employment where they felt appreciated and valued.

Shortly after losing my best employees, I got into a project worth about $4,000,000 in downtown Baltimore. I ended up spending $3,000,000 of my own money that was not part of the contract work. When I completed the work and the client and developer reimbursed me, they denied my change order and sent me into a Chapter 7 complete bankruptcy.

In the first quarter of 2013, I lost my home, all my money, all of my assets, most of my family and friends, and I ended up moving to Raleigh, North Carolina in April with $400 to my name. When I got there I had both of my cars repossessed on the same day. I was in a bad mental health space from my bankruptcy; I got fired from two jobs in the same week, and I was at rock bottom, or so I thought.

I worked odd jobs to pay the bills. In September 2013, I took a job as a custodian working in downtown Raleigh, making $8.25 an hour. One day on my shift I ended up having my rock bottom moment of clarity, when someone's garbage full of rotten meat, spoiled milk, and other nasty protruding garbage got all over my body, skin, and clothes. I cleaned myself up and sat on the curb by the dumpster. I put my head in my hands and cried. I realized that everything that happened to me in my life was because I was an arrogant, horrible, egomaniac leader. I vowed at that moment if I ever got my life back on track, that I would never again let my ego ruin my life and that I would always remain humble.

That morning I came home and sat at my desk and wrote out what my three biggest strengths were, and decided I was going to be a keynote speaker. I launched my career in September 2013, and for two and a half years, I did not get one paid job. That entire time, I was not trying to be a good leader. I was not trying to serve a cause greater than myself. I was not trying to help others. I was trying to make money, and I was only focused on what I needed and wanted.

In 2016, I learned how to serve and help others, use my mess and turn it into a powerful message. I started learning how to be a leader. Finally, in April, I landed my first paid speaking job, and that, along with the new mindset I developed on how to be a true leader, propelled me forward.

I continued to work on my craft. I continued to better myself. I continued to learn how to put others needs before mine, and in the last five and a half years, I have worked for 27 Fortune 500 Brands. I am a coach, a consultant, an author, a podcast host and have completely turned my life around. And I owe all of it to learning how to be a humble servant leader, instead of an egomaniac trying to intimidate and scare others.

You may be asking yourself, "Marques, how can I become a better leader?" And the answer is quite simple; learn how to serve others. The best leaders learn how to be a leader by serving others around them. If you want to break it down further, you need to learn how to be proficient in these four areas: Sensemaking, Relating, Visioning, and Inventing.

These four areas are crucial in learning how to serve others and be the "rock" they need in times of uncertainty. Another area to learn is how to be great as a leader; you need to know how to respond and not react in high intense pressure situations. The best leaders can think and be strategic and tactical under pressure, and they know how to calm others on the team. This is another area you want to continue to grow in as you charge forward into being a servant leader.

Let's recap. You have taken the first step toward being the servant leader that you desire to be. You have displayed discipline and focus on doing and being your best, which is phenomenal. Now it is time to do the hard work. It is time to create a strategic and tactical plan to help you get from where you are to where you want to be; time to dig deep and work on improving sensemaking, relating, visioning, and inventing. It's time to dig in, get in the trenches with your team members, and work alongside them to take them where they want to go. Notice I said "take them" and not show them, not tell them, but take them!

The best servant leaders take people to heights they never thought possible. They walk the walk right alongside their team members and take them to where they need to be. So now that you have this knowledge, how are you going to apply it? One of my favorite quotes I came up with is, "Knowledge is power, but applying knowledge is life changing."

So go out and take command of your journey and help others do the same.

Truly global leadership: Exploring the world for new ideas, insights and inspirations

By Jeremy Solomons
Kigali City, Rwanda

"We never know the reality of things: We see only what we are aware of. It is our consciousness that determines the shape of the world around us—its size, motion and meaning." Nawal El Saadawi, Egyptian feminist and writer.

Over 20 years ago, former General Electric CEO Jack Welch said, "The Jack Welch of the future cannot be like me." Today, we still base much global leadership development on research and ideas emanating from Europe and North America.

Great work is undoubtedly still being done on both continents, but if leadership is genuinely global, now would seem to be the right time to challenge any long-standing traditions and expectations. We should break free from self-imposed limitations, expand horizons, and listen to the 90% of the world's population who live beyond the Northern Atlantic shores, and harbor many sources of global leadership ideas, insight and inspiration—both ancient and modern. Here is a small selection from across the globe and from across time.

Around 2,500 years ago, it was Lao Tzu, a Chinese philosopher and author of the Tao Te Ching, who foreshadowed modern-day communitarian and servant leadership when he said, "A leader is best when people barely know he exists when his work is done, his aim fulfilled, they will say: we did it ourselves."

Likewise, his contemporary Siddhartha Gautama, predated the current focus on mindfulness and self-leadership with such words as, "The mind is everything. What you think, you become." and, "Peace comes from within. Do not seek it without."

More recently, there was the fearless Ashanti Queen Mother, Yaa Asantewaa, in modern-day Ghana. Her call to arms against British colonialism in the late 19th century inspired more recent trends in women's leadership, "If you, the men of Asante, will not go forward, then we will. We, the women, will. I shall call upon my fellow women. We will fight the white men. We will fight till the last of us falls on the battlefield."

The words of individual leaders instruct and motivate traditional concepts within societies and cultures outside Europe and North America, are fundamental to their modern ways of being, thinking, acting, and leading.

In Mexico and other Spanish-speaking countries, people talk about Respeto, which loosely translates as respect, but this does not fully capture all the nuances of this traditional cultural value and how it relates to leadership.

Respeto is more than respecting others. It is a conscious awareness of the relative layers of hierarchy and authority and knowing the precise obedience, deference, courtesy, and public behavior required in a situation concerning people of a particular age, gender, or social status. Sometimes, it could show up in something as simple as to who you say "good morning" to at the office, and how and when.

In Japan, there is Nemawashi, which means laying the groundwork. But it is more than that. It is a gardening term that literally means, "binding up the roots" for transplanting a tree. In Japan, an arborist would take great care to cut and clean each root, neatly wrapping them up, ensuring that we fully prepared the tree to thrive in its new location. Likewise, a Japanese leader would smooth the way for any large-scale change by conducting unofficial pre-meetings. Unofficial pre-meetings get input from the ground up before the formal meeting, to discuss and confirm consensus on the proposal, ensuring no big surprises, or broken branches.

Many already know about the Nguni Bantu term Ubuntu, which is usually translated as: "I am because we are". This powerful concept relates to humanity, community, interconnectedness and togetherness. South African leaders and influencers have consciously embodied it, such as Nelson Mandela, his daughter Zindzi and Archbishop Desmond Tutu, who once said, "We need other human beings in order to be human."

Another less well-known term outside South Africa was relevant during the Covid pandemic when the need for compassionate leadership came to the fore. The Zulu word Sawubona literally means "I (or we) see you" highlighting the importance of recognizing other people's innate and deep worthiness, dignity and honor. The usual response is: Yebo, Sawubona or "I (or we) see you too."

And here in Rwanda, where I live, there is the traditional and practical, collective leadership concept of Umuganda, or Community Service, revived after the 1994 Genocide against the Tutsis. Before the Covid pandemic, the country of Rwanda would shut down on the last Saturday morning of each month to allow villages, neighborhoods and streets to come together in public service such as fixing an elderly person's roof, clearing clogged drains or building a community center, as examples.

No single continent, country, culture, institution or thinker has the right answer or prescription for what makes a truly global leader. But it would seem wise for both current and emerging global leaders to free themselves from any preconceived notions of success, and look beyond the obvious and familiar to discover a whole world of ideas, insight, and inspiration. Or, in the words of the 13th century Persian poet Rumi, "Why do you stay in prison when the door is so wide open?"

My breakthrough story of leadership

By John Whaley
Houston, Texas

In my pursuit to find peace of mind, the focus on leadership became the cornerstone of living my best life. Sports provided my first formal lesson in leadership. I was selected as a team captain and I earned the starting varsity quarterback position during my high school senior year. Recalling the experiences of others taught me the potential downfall of acting like the hustler, go-getter, boss, king, leader, overachiever, or star. That "all about me" mindset others possessed and flaunted more than not, left them isolated and their potential capped.

As a newly appointed leader of 10 people on the football field, I knew my team had to trust, appreciate, and support one another. The role required me to push past my potential and help each team member in their journey to be their absolute best. Leadership during practice sessions meant finding my WAR dogs! The phrase Ready, Able, and Willing (RAW) changed my mindset early in life. My goal was to connect with the Willing players with strong Abilities then get them Ready (WAR) during each practice and off-field encounter.

A player that lacks sufficient willingness would likely not transition to a leadership mindset. As a team, reaching the next level required a high level of earned trust, fluid communication, and a passion for personal improvement.

Game time leadership required each of us to reinforce the day's vision, purpose, and mission. We knew our adversaries were not just eleven disparate people on the other side of the ball. Instead, we battled the energy of an entire team of 50 plus people, besides their fans, coaches, and game officials. I trusted my co-captains to help encourage and nurture a team spirit of independent thinking around collaborative actions. This mindset, culture, and set of team norms allowed our team to win the conference championship and reach the state's final four. We were the unknowns from a shrinking school of 850 students in a rural town, that battled and beat schools with graduating senior classes three times the size of our entire student body that season.

This primary lesson in leadership paved the way for many other opportunities to grow as a person and leader. I have outlined my top 11 lessons learned from the last 30 years.

1. My mindset around leadership focuses strongly on productivity and outcomes first. I must win before I can teach others to win. Wins are any step forward.

2. Leadership is the act of removing unnecessary obstacles out of the pathway of rising (WAR) leaders. I measure my success as a leader based on those I mentor, coach, and advise. I apply resources that build a better understanding of how others think, feel, and react.

3. Binding individuals around a cause, mission, goal, or thought is about articulating the pathway and expected outcome unique to each person involved.

4. Developing future leaders requires an ongoing commitment to self-improvement in the areas of personal and social awareness. Pursue what you don't know and connect with those you don't quite understand.

5. Leadership culture embraces an ecosystem for less talk and more productiveness, communication, collaboration, wins, advancements, innovation, effectiveness, efficiency, and engagement.

6. Influencers and entertainers motivate and inspire people; leaders connect with and elevate those driven to do more with life.

7. Setbacks as a leader taught me that everyone does not have the will to grow and lead. I can't pull people up; they can only hold me down, so I strive to be the best me and pave the way for those aspiring to rise higher. The goal is to develop those willing and ready to level up in any area of life.

8. My work/life harmony motto is thinking big, planning small, and enjoying everything in between. Surround yourself with people that are living their best life. Research the frameworks, resources, and people that support and build strong leaders. There is no right or wrong in our universe, only outcomes and consequences for our actions. Explore and engage while you are able; you cannot fail, you only build on the lessons learned.

9. Stay current and connected to others through technology and techniques that articulate your purpose, passion, and pathway. I have explored many resources, from broadcast radio and television to the latest online video conference tools to connect with others in a meaningful and intentional way. Be mindful.

10. Sharing is caring, and the art of mentoring is my second important cornerstone. Regardless of circumstances, the proper insight can change your path exponentially. I have mentored, coached, and advised thousands of people since 2001, and each session led to a deeper and more meaningful thought exchange. Mentoring fosters a strategic mindset around the desired outcome, while coaching develops the tactical resources to move forward.

11. Last, leading from purpose. Be the curious one and explore new areas. Work to understand and be understood. Establishing your purpose requires a clear and concise target, consensus on the threat, and overcoming the pathway. The explicit purpose creates meaningful daily habits that ground your ability to build a solid foundation for significant and measured progress.

Leadership skills improve with meaningful efforts and timely evaluations. The people following or shadowing a leader's guidance experience various changes in their purpose. Leaders must maintain awareness and flexibility in their approach to supporting and mentoring for success.

Rising and aspiring leaders rarely need encouragement; they need frameworks, principles, and examples. I live my life to the fullest and share the mindset, skillset, and toolset to reach new heights. I support others by helping them reframe how they see their potential.

Communication

Voices for Leadership: Lessons from the operating room and the orchestra pit

By Eileen McDargh, CEO The Resiliency Group
Dana Point, California

When Brian created *Voices for Leadership*, I became intrigued by the word "for."

It implies individuals who speak out in voices that show leadership, voices that beckon others to follow, and voices that offer wisdom for all who seek to contribute to the world.

Leadership is not about profit margins, C-suite holders, or a ranking in the Fortune 100—though indeed that could be the result. It's about listening to what these voices offer.

"Leadership comes from a place that troubles your heart."

Years ago, those words leapt off the page of a monthly American business magazine, from an article profiling the work of Dr. G. Venkataswamy, founder of Aravind Eye Clinic—the largest eye clinic in the world. What troubled Dr. V. was blindness caused by cataracts—the single largest cause of blindness around the world; and preventable.

The story of Dr. V. and Aravind reads like an epic tale. Dr. V. received his medical degree from Stanley Medical College, Chennai, in 1944. He joined the Indian Army Medical Corps but had to retire in 1948 after developing rheumatoid arthritis. The condition became so severe that he was bedridden for over a year. He struggled even to walk and could not hold a pen in his crippled fingers.

Despite his condition, he returned to medical school and earned his diploma and master's degree in ophthalmology. Through his hard work and determination, Dr. V. learned how to hold a scalpel and perform cataract surgery. Eventually, he performed over 100 surgeries a day and over 100,000 successful eye surgeries during his lifetime. Today, 14 hospitals span India, along with specialty clinics, physician training, and product development. His voice for leadership said, "I am troubled, and I must do something." His voice was about action.

What troubles your heart? It doesn't have to be as earth-shattering as curing blindness, but voices for leadership say, "I must do something." What might you do?

This next voice for leadership doesn't come from being troubled, but from falling in love with the work and the workers. Here is a scenario.

Imagine a crusty group of seasoned professionals standing, applauding, and cheering a 28-year-old leader who has turned a same-old same-old product into something fresh and exciting. This does not happen—particularly when the professionals are members of the Israel Philharmonic. But under the baton of young maestro Gustavo Dudamel, orchestra members did.

Southern California music lovers are now witnessing the same magic of a man who started as a tot playing the violin in El Sistema, the publicly funded program for primarily disadvantaged children in Venezuela. As conductor of the Los Angeles Philharmonic, Dudamel's musical genius fills the Hollywood Bowl and his voice for leadership loudly echoes. To Dudamel, music is a vehicle for social change, but—as his orchestra members insist—he brings something more to the work scene: LOVE.

In a recent interview, Dudamel's leadership genius jumped off the page as something that leaders in all industries can practice. The secret: Love the music and the musicians who play it.

Dudamel makes every player a star, asking them to play their best and then—just a little more and still more. He is a persistent and disciplined communicator. He delivers the same message, evoking over and over the possibility of amazing outcomes, and a belief in the individual strength of each player that becomes better when joined with others.

He uses the power of words to express the results he seeks. It's not the language of the bottom line and shareholder return, but words that turn a symphony into human terms: Blood, meat, happiness, magic. Every player can sense an emotional component in the result.

Imagine what would happen if leaders could vocalize about a product or a service, turning it into something that resonates emotionally with team members. I can make a case for software technicians as surely as a team of surgical nurses.

According to close observers, Dudamel's eyes radiate joy and energy when working with the orchestra. He admits that having fun with the "product" and the players allows him to create a musical experience that brings the "buyers" of the product and the "makers" of the product to their feet.

Fun. Energy. Joy. These aren't words that one associates with work. Results without joy, fun (however one defines it), and energy create a disengaged workforce and a perfunctory leadership style.

Do you listen to your internal voice asking what gives you energy and joy about your work? Would your teammates and colleagues say that you display energy and joy in your work? What might it take?

As for Dr. V. and eyesight-saving surgery, he passed away in 2006, but the joy his former staff feel with each successful operation generates the energy to continue his amazing work.

Now more than ever, we yearn to hear voices FOR leadership. As Nobel Prize winner Malala Yousafzal fiercely stated, "When the whole world is silent, even one voice becomes powerful."

The value of one-on-one meetings

By Chris Allen

Charlotte, North Carolina

The employee quit rate in the US has been steadily rising for over a decade. Employees are increasingly dissatisfied in the workplace. In 2011, a Gallup Poll report titled *The Economics of Wellbeing*, found that only 12% of employees strongly agreed that they have a substantially higher overall wellbeing because of their employer. Gallup's *State of the Global Workplace: 2021 Report* shows that only 20% of employees are engaged in the workplace. Other surveys show a disconnect between the next generation (41 years old and younger), of what they want, and of what the employer believes they want.

McKinsey & Company released a study in September 2021, highlighting the disconnect between what employees want and what employers think employees want. McKinsey & Company identified that what's important to employees is the organization, manager, and sense of belonging within the company. Employers believe employees are looking for "transactional" benefits, like compensation and perks, while employees are more likely to prioritize "relational" benefits. This is a chasmic disconnect. So, what kind of culture would attract and keep people? According to the data, a culture where people feel value and a sense of belonging. Value and belonging are experienced through relationships. The next generation needs the relational impact of a leader who invests in people.

The leadership skills necessary to attract, motivate, develop, and retain people are not being taught. People are leaving organizations where those skills are not a priority. Many organizations promote high potential individual contributors to management positions, with little training in leading people. Career advancement emphasizes transactional benefits rather than relational ones. But there is a straightforward practice that could solve many issues in the workplace. Gallup and other sources confirm that consistent feedback is meaningful, motivating, and increases engagement. They found consistent feedback occurs in the one-on-one meeting; therefore, the value of a regular one-on-one meeting cannot be over-emphasized. So, why aren't one-on-one meetings prioritized? There are a couple of reasons.

First, leaders may not understand how important it is to take the time. Many leaders will choose an excuse to rationalize why they do not have time for one-on-ones. Many high-performing leaders see a one-on-one as competing for their time. Remember, we've taken high-performing individual contributors and made them managers. They are recognized and rewarded for their ability to get stuff done, accomplish tasks, and exceed expectations. Why would they change this learned behavior, sacrificing the reward they've always experienced? It requires a change of belief and habit. If leaders believe a one-on-one provides the ability to accomplish more, by delegating or redistributing tasks, the time will be prioritized. If leaders see the ROI and the personal benefit of a one-on-one meeting, they will prioritize its consistency into a habit.

Second, managers fear not knowing what to talk about or making the conversation valuable and productive. Some leaders view a one-on-one as "catch-up" time and therefore do not recognize its full value. It is more than an update and is simpler than leaders realize. Here is a simple outline for one-on-one conversations. The Three C's: *Context, Challenges,* and *Commitments* frame a model for these valuable conversations.

Context: This is where leaders discuss what is going on with the individual's personal and professional life. By asking simple questions, leaders will better understand their employees. Here are two suggestions to get started: How are you doing? What would you like to discuss today? The point is to find out how they are feeling. These questions show you value them and care enough to listen. The insights gleaned from these conversations will help you understand the person, their strengths and weaknesses, their motivations and how to help them become a better version of themselves. Context also sets the stage for how the meeting proceeds.

Challenges: This is where leaders discuss the challenges an individual is experiencing professionally and allow the leader to discuss their challenges. Here are some questions to create engagement: What's going on? What is getting in the way? What is your history with this? What's your goal? How can I help you? By regularly entering this conversation, trust is built between two individuals. The need to prepare for "difficult conversations" diminishes as accountability becomes a regular part of each one-on-one. As the relationship grows and trust increases, individuals will allow you to hold them accountable and will willingly accept feedback.

Commitments: Both parties commit and agree to follow through on the discussion. Here are examples of questions to confirm commitment: What could you do to move forward? How would the wisest person you know solve this? How likely are you to do what you have said? By synthesizing the conversation and establishing a settlement on the commitments made on both sides, they established clarity in expectations. Individuals feel valued when they learn how to "win" especially when their leader commits to following up at the next meeting. These conversations around the Three C's establish the expectations for success.

If one-on-one meetings become a consistent leadership expectation within organizations, we can solve many of the issues creating attrition. Organizations can understand what employees need by listening. If an individual has regular one-on-one conversations with their manager (based on the Three C's), they feel valued, feel a sense of belonging, and hear tangible feedback for growth. Growth encourages us to become self-actualized. Successful one-on-ones can help individuals become a better version of themselves, which is the inherent value.

Value one-on-ones, and people will feel valued.

Defining servant leadership and building champions of service

By Wes Dove

Harrisonburg, Virginia

Robert K. Greenleaf coined the modern idea of servant leadership in an essay he published in 1970 called *The Servant as Leader*. In explaining the idea, Greenleaf shared, "It begins with the natural feeling that one wants to serve, to serve first. Then conscious choice brings one to aspire to lead. That person is sharply different from one who is the leader first..."

A decade later, as a kid in Sunday school, I learned about the idea of servant leadership through stories about a carpenter who became a teacher, determined to make sure that the folks who came to hear him were fed before they started their long journey home.

As I looked deeper into the idea, I found a post on the Society for Human Resource Management (SHRM) website called *The Art of Servant Leadership*. The post explained, "The servant leader moves beyond the transactional aspects of management, and instead actively seeks to develop and align an employee's sense of purpose with the company mission." This same article tied servant leadership back to early Eastern culture, citing Laozi, a 5th-century

Chinese philosopher suggesting that, "When the best leaders finished their work, their people would say: we did it ourselves."

Regardless of where your initial exposure to the idea of servant leadership came from, knowing what it means and applying it to what you do are two different things! In the business environment today, we're under intense pressure to deliver return on investment—and that can make us feel like our best immediate option is to bark orders and crack the proverbial whip. But I've never seen that approach yield anything more than short-term results, if that.

In an Ottawa University article called *5 Proven Characteristics of a Servant Leader*, the author seemed to have that same belief when they shared that, "There is a mountain of statistical evidence linked to the proven effectiveness of leaders who have mastered the aforementioned (servant leadership) traits."

In *The Servant*, James C. Hunter shares that, "A leader is someone who recognizes and meets the legitimate needs of their people, and removes all the barriers so they can serve the customer." He says, "To lead, you must serve."

As with anything else we do in life, simply knowing something is only the beginning; we can't expect to achieve real results until we take action on that knowledge. This is where the rubber meets the road! But even when we're taking action with the best of intentions, there will be times when a team member's perception of whether we're serving them is indeed their reality. To "meet the legitimate needs of our people," as Hunter suggested, we not only need to recognize those needs, we also need to perform the service in a way that matters to them.

Over the last decade, I've been able to help dozens of organizations build strong communication into their cultures by implementing tools based on William Marston's work on *The DISC Model of Human Behavior*. One of the core tenants I've shared with each company has been the idea of The Platinum Rule. Everyone I meet has a foundational understanding of The Golden Rule; do unto others as we'd have them do unto us. The Platinum Rule for effective communication tells us to, "communicate with others as THEY want us to communicate with them" rather than how we want them to communicate with us. While that may seem like semantics, the difference is critical once we've invested the time into learning to recognize the primary communication styles of the surrounding team. If we apply this same approach to serving each of our team members, we can significantly increase the odds of having their perceptions match our reality. After all, if they don't perceive what we're doing as serving them, are we leading them?

Once we've developed this approach ourselves, we compound our results throughout our entire organization by teaching this thought process to everyone else on our team who carries leadership responsibility. It requires us to provide a visible example of the behaviors we need to duplicate. We'll also need to empower our leaders to take action with their team members as they see fit to serve the needs they're recognizing. Then we'll need to be sure to provide what I've heard Jeff Henderson call alliance feedback, as we guide and mentor them.

I'm not suggesting that this will be an easy or an immediate process, with results showing up right away. I've seen nothing of value that works that way. But I have seen the process of defining—and living out—servant leadership to create a culture that builds real champions of service. Even though the effort can be significant, the juice will absolutely be worth the squeeze!

Empathy: A missing voice in our workspaces

By Joseph T. Dutkiewicz
Lakeland, Florida

Wednesday started like any other workday until somewhere between my morning routine and my drive to work, I received a call from the nursing home. "Your dad has taken a fall and has a skin tear on his wrist. When the staff moved him from the bed to the wheelchair, his foot wrapped around the footplate, and he went hard down to the floor." After the call, I felt overwhelmed and unable to do enough to protect my dad.

As the eldest child, I became guardian and conservator for both of my parents. They were facing reduced mobility and self-care in their 70's. I knew I couldn't take care of them and work as well. Now, how do I keep my father safe from the tumbles and bruises of Parkinson's and his lack of ability to communicate.

It weighed heavily on me as I arrived late at the office.

The top priority for the day was a release of an analysis and recommendation to be shared with upper management. I tried to share with my boss why I was late because he didn't read my text. He greeted me with, "I don't want to hear about it. Get to work. I had to step in to get your team moving. We now need to review it in 30 minutes." My boss never looked at my earlier text, my need to share. All I needed was an ear in order to reset.

Have you felt similar loneliness when a day turned upside down, where you needed someone to listen and were rejected without a glance? According to the *2021 State of Workplace Empathy Study*, performed by Businessolver. com, only one in four people felt their leaders offered "satisfactory" care and understanding.

Microsoft earlier this year shared their *2021 Work Trend Index* of 30,000 workers in 31 countries that showed over 40% were considering leaving their job. Generation Z workers were closer to 54%.

Teams have become more siloed, and digital exhaustion is a real and unsustainable threat. Further, 37% say their employer is asking too much of them. One in five employers doesn't care about their work-life balance, while meetings and after-hour chats continue to climb each week.

In April, May and June 2021, 11.5 million people quit their jobs. After the COVID lockdown, media reports began reporting that restaurant and other front-facing customer service staff left without notice, and that businesses were moving to reduced service, unable to staff their operations while the economy was opening back up.

A few suggest we should think of it in terms of a Great Realignment—a realignment with what is important and learned during the 2020 lockdown. The most cited in conversations is a desire to do something meaningful; be in a more collaborative environment, get away from negative bosses and co-workers, and high expectations meant to cleanse the "laggards" and punish the "stars." The virtual and hybrid boundaries need strengthening from the constant 24/7 depression and exhaustion. Recorded clicks and always-on cameras don't even get close to what people are experiencing.

People share feelings of not knowing their team members and feeling isolated from conversations with those in the office. Hannah McConnaughey, Product Marketing Manager at Microsoft, shared in the *Work Trend Index Report* that, "Without hallway conversations, chance encounters, and small talk over coffee, it's hard to feel connected even to my immediate team, much less build meaningful connections across the company." Some relish looking into people's homes through the webcam and hope to see something in common. They hope to learn more about the others in their teams. We can do better.

Daniel Goleman, noted psychologist and founder of Emotional Intelligence in management, noted that within the four domains where our emotions lie: self-awareness, self-management, social awareness and relationship management, there are 12 core competencies.

I suggest the missing voice, and sometimes overlooked, the empathy in Goleman's social awareness. When we understand and manage our own emotions, we have room to go beyond ourselves to understand others' emotions and the challenges they face.

When leaders, that's you and me, have influence with others, and effectively use empathy, we create deeper bonds of trust and loyalty with those we lead.

What turns around the current dynamic in the workspace? What can you do to make a difference and be a better leader? Here are a few better forward steps I use to employ empathy, which I learned from conversations with clients, friends, and peers leading teams.

1. Get comfortable – Are you able to distance yourself from the myriad of distractions to focus on what the other person is telling you?

2. Get higher listening – What is the other person saying and not saying about the situation they face?

3. Get validating – Authentically offer that you understand the situation they face and offer, "How can I help?"

4. Get compassionate – It is not a one-and-done type of thing. Periodically check-in through an informal chat. Send a note of appreciation for what they are doing great.

5. Get observing – Focus on the mental morale of the team or the individual. "Is my team burning out, overwhelmed, blocked from proceeding forward? How can I lighten their load?"

People have only been bringing parts of themselves to work—the parts they feel they can show to fit in with the team. What is hiding may need attention and presents itself when least expected. Are you ready to open the door, stop what you are doing, and focus on the person in front of you?

Not all people are lacking in empathy. In fact, we each have it. You may not be aware that you have practiced empathy before. It is a learned skill and takes repetition to master. At a recent leadership event in Lakeland, Florida the afternoon panel of selected small business leaders offered their perspective on how empathy is on their minds with each decision they make. In the decision process, they each felt ownership to care for the people that worked for them. "How does this decision affect my team and their families?"

We can find empathy, though we think it has to be the boss. Sometimes it is a co-worker. People are noting across the globe that there is a lot of room for improvement to live empathetically in the workspace and create more caring cultures. It has to start with each of us stepping up. Will you join me in employing the missing voice of empathy in the leadership of your workspace?

How to build culture

By Tyzer Evans
Katy, Texas

Company culture makes or breaks a business. At the core of any business, success or failure depend on how leaders make their people feel when they show up to do their job. After spending the last 15 years managing some of the largest companies in the world, I have found a few common themes on what works exceptionally well and what does not, when building a great work culture where people want to show up.

I will cover five pillars that I believe if you can execute, you will completely change the feeling, production and increase happiness in your work culture.

Mission driven

The first important step to building a great culture is making sure everyone understands the company's mission. The only time an employee hears about a company's mission is when they start; this is wrong. Your mission, and your core values are things you should come back to often, very often. You want everyone within your organization not only to understand your mission, your goal, and your why, you also want them to know how they are contributing.

The more someone feels like they are a part of the collective, and they clearly understand how they contribute, the more they will execute their work with pride and precision. One way I felt like I have been able to drive home the mission with flawless execution is to have a daily meeting. A daily session of 15 to 30 minutes sets the tone and gets everyone on the same page.

I plan my schedule out for a month, so I have relevant topics prepared but also have fun with them! Sometimes I will have a meeting where everyone says one thing they are grateful for about another teammate. Some mornings I will bring up a struggle that someone has had during the week, and let everyone brainstorm on a solution; other times I might play a motivational video. I can tell you that if you do this consistently and relay these meeting topics back to your mission, you will have set yourself up for much more success.

Teamwork makes the dream work

The second step is to identify if everyone is on your team or "bus" and are they in the right seats? Before we discuss who is sitting where, I find it valuable to understand your team's energy. Do you have someone who is constantly disrupting the energy in the office? Someone who is engaging in drama or stirring the pot? If someone like this exists on the team, I like to meet with them and give them a second chance and be brutally honest about their perception in the office. Most will turn it around, but if not, move on and get them out.

Now we need to make sure that everyone on the bus is sitting in the right seat. One of my favorite stories to tell is of a struggling sales rep. He worked hard, did what I asked, always smiled, and believed in the company and what we were trying to do, but sales were not for him. I explained how valuable he was to the organization and thought it would suit his caring nature to be in a different role. He agreed and made the move. He became the number one retention person. Right person, wrong seat. Make sure you don't cut loose good people who were placed in the wrong seat!

Goals

The third thing to do is sit down with everyone who is a direct report and ask them to write out between three to five personal and professional goals.

Only three percent of people write their goals. Even less follow through on them. Here is a huge opportunity to understand what motivates your people, and a chance to get better buy-in and develop loyalty.

After they have their goals down, meet with them one-on-one and help them draw a roadmap to accomplishing these goals. Once the road map is set, allow 30 minutes to meet with everyone once a month to review their goals and help them track their progress, and keep them accountable. They will thank you when they see results in parts of their lives in and outside of work. We all want to be around those who support and encourage us. There is no better way than helping someone accomplish goals they didn't even know they had.

Empower your people

Fourth, empower your people. For the first 90 days, you need to be hands on. You need to make sure they are getting the feel of your company, that they can trust that you are there for them and want to see them succeed. Setting a written outline for their first 30, 60 and 90 days is a great way to keep you and the new employee on the same page.

As they become more tenured, let go of your control. People don't like micromanagement; they want responsibility, knowing that they contribute and feel empowered. Companies with a toxic culture micro-manage their people.

And when they win, celebrate. Empowering your people will 10x your results and company culture.

Fun

Fifth, have fun! We all have to work, so we don't want our people showing up dreading it. I have always hated the saying, "It's almost Friday" or "Another day closer to Friday." What kind of life is that? You want a culture where people aren't looking forward to Friday; they are looking forward to Monday. Celebrate team wins together, celebrate company milestones, and do activities that promote team bonding, i.e., golf, escape rooms, taco Tuesday, etc. There are plenty of activities you can do throughout the year that won't break the bank.

Leading during uncertain times

By Brian Gallagher

Greenville, South Carolina

Change is a constant in life. As leaders, we have a responsibility to be trusted beacons amidst constant change. We decide in an increasingly uncertain, complex, and ambiguous (VUCA) world. While these factors complicate decision-making, humble and transparent leaders who embrace a collaborative, creative, and agile approach will successfully navigate uncertainty.

Based on the leadership theories of authors Warren Bennis and Burt Nanus, the term VUCA was first used in 1987 and stands for Volatility, Uncertainty, Complexity and Ambiguity. The US Army War College embraced the term to describe the military challenges in a post-Soviet era. Military leaders no longer had a single enemy on which to focus, but faced many threats that required different ways of thinking, seeing, and reacting.

VUCA describes the situation of constant, unpredictable change indicative of an environment in business today. Labor and workforce shortages, supply chain interruptions, rising costs, social change and political, economic, and regulatory uncertainty are some factors all leaders face.

Building trust

Challenging times require leaders to embrace an increased level of collaboration, communication, creativity, and flexibility. Leaders don't have to have all the answers. They must provide a vision and create a sense of stability. It's okay for leaders to feel fear; after all, we are human too. People have a high expectation and turn to leaders for reassurance and guidance. They want to develop a sense of certainty based on trusting their leaders.

Each year, a global communications firm, Edelman, releases its Edelman Trust Barometer. The Trust Barometer is an annual study of trust and credibility. For 21 years, the Trust Barometer has been a valuable tool, helping leaders understand perceptions and where there are gaps in trust. The results provide clear insights into what actions organizations can take to help build trust. The recent Trust Barometer shows trust in leaders is at all-time lows, and reveals an epidemic of misinformation and widespread mistrust of societal institutions and leaders. While this is concerning, it is an opportunity to lead.

Trust in leaders comes from competence, ethical behavior, and personal experience. In challenging times, people look to leaders to help them make sense of changing business conditions, and to equip employees with the tools to help them handle changing situations.

Navigating change

While the vision for your organization remains constant, the path to fulfilling that vision will probably change in the face of uncertainty. Leaders have beliefs and a set of core values from which they lead. These core values help shape and influence decision-making. While the values must remain constant, uncertainty requires leaders to develop different approaches, scenarios, and contingency plans. Constantly monitoring situations, engaging with your team, and discussing how external conditions affect your organization are critical.

Acknowledge that outcomes will not be certain

Defining reality and acknowledging uncertainty will help build trust and confidence with team members. Leaders should recognize the journey will be difficult and describe the approach they will take without guaranteeing outcomes.

Seek different points of view

Leaders may have limited ability to gain perspectives in different situations. Engaging with others to gain insights and perspectives provokes creative thinking, improves our ability to learn, grow, and effectively navigate the complexity of the business world.

Inform, connect, and guide.

Consistently communicating vision and direction is a hallmark of a great leader. In uncertain times, remaining on message is critical. Fear results from not understanding and not knowing what lies ahead. People want leaders that share where the organization is heading and honesty about its future. Often, this requires tough conversations. Effective leaders who are transparent, open, and speak with clarity and intent are the most effective at engaging employees and building trust.

Be humble

Naturally, leaders want to have the answers and seek solutions that protect their position, status, or ego. Usually, this mindset closes the mind to courses of action that might not be the best for the organization. While leaders need to lead with confidence, being humble is critical. A good leader is humble, and the best leaders will show their vulnerability. By leading from a place of humility, we can learn and see the best course of action for the team, not only for the leader. Even admitting you are not sure of the outcome will help build trust with your team. Being humble and vulnerable builds trust.

In the shadow of constant disruptive forces, leaders today face many new and unprecedented challenges. When seas are calm, anyone can sail a ship, but it takes a leader to chart the course and navigate when the seas are rough. In a volatile, changing, and uncertain world, humility, transparency, agility and a collaborative mindset lead organizations. Leaders must pursue trust and engagement with the same rigor, intent, passion, and energy to deliver on profits.

Leading in times of crisis: Facing challenges every day

By Dr. Kim Moore

Tampa, Florida

Have you found yourself in a situation when you were unprepared? While many crises are minor and leaders can respond quickly based on previous experiences, there will be times when leaders must step into unknown territory.

As a leader, I've found myself in many situations where I wasn't sure what to do. I remember my first leadership position as a junior leader. I was excited but also concerned, wondering if I could handle the unique challenges that would arise.

To prepare for my first leadership opportunity, I met with my mentor. During the meeting, my mentor peppered me with questions as we worked through different leadership scenarios. As we concluded our session, my mentor gave me a piece of advice that I still follow today.

So, what was my mentor's advice? She said, "The choices you make today will determine your future success." As I sat there with a perplexed look on my face, my mentor explained the benefits and challenges of leadership.

While there are many benefits of leadership, there are also challenges. One common fear is dealing with problematic people. In addition, delegation can also be a challenge for leaders. My mentor emphasized the biggest challenge of leadership was responding to unexpected situations. She told me every leader would face multiple crises, and if I made good choices, I would rise above the circumstances to lead myself and others.

As a leader, I have experienced many good days, for example, when everyone showed up for work or the perfectly performed plan. But I have also experienced many bad days, like when my computer crashed moments before a presentation to my boss's boss, or when half of my leadership team was sick with the flu. So while leadership is a privilege full of excellent opportunities to add value to others, it is also full of challenging situations.

As a leader, I am confident you have experienced good and bad days. But you may wonder if you will ever face a significant crisis? It's not a question of if you'll find yourself in a crisis; it's a question of when. The real question is how will you lead yourself and your team?

So, if a bad day, week, or month is not a crisis, what qualifies? According to John Maxwell, "A crisis is several consecutive bad days that you can't walk away from. A crisis is an intense time of difficulty requiring a decision that will be a turning point." Using Maxwell's definition, your decisions during a crisis can hurt or improve the situation.

One of my favorite quotes from Winston Churchill is, "Never let a good crisis go to waste." I love this quote because it reminds me that there are opportunities for people to grow, possibilities for making changes, and chances to strengthen your organization amid a crisis. Therefore, as the leader, it is pivotal for you to make good choices.

Every leader will face multiple crises. When you find yourself in a crisis, you have a choice on how to respond. So how do you, as a leader, rise to the occasion? Consider the following six strategies to help guide you.

- Keep the main thing the main thing. Define the root cause of the crisis. During a crisis, it is easy to get sidetracked by distractions. So instead, remove the distractions and stay focused on the main thing.
- Adapt to uncertainty. You are the leader, and everyone will look to you for direction and encouragement. Flexibility is a leader's best friend. So, it's okay to acknowledge you don't know the answer, but don't allow yourself to get stuck in the chaos. Instead, take time to work through the issues and proactively move toward solutions.

- Communicate and delegate. Leaders set the direction for the organization and must be visible and communicate with clarity. The people you lead want to see and connect with their leaders, especially during difficult times. Delegating specific tasks to team members during a crisis will help keep them focused on solutions and purpose.

- Align decisions with your values. Stress can adversely affect a person's thinking and behavior. Grounding your choices in your values will keep you on track when you are under pressure. Amid the chaos of a crisis, you will be pulled in many directions; staying on track will move you toward solutions faster.

- Give grace and compassion. People are a leader's most valuable resource, so recognize the impact of stress on your team. Tuning in to the needs of your team is vital. Remember, people will make mistakes under pressure, so extend grace and compassion throughout the crisis.

- Take care of your team and yourself. The wellbeing of your team is essential. Schedule a time to check in with team members. Create a regular schedule for the team to bond together on a personal level. As a leader, you cannot give what you don't have; therefore, you must care for yourself. Refresh and re-energize with activities like exercising, knitting, or reading.

Implementing these strategies will give you greater peace and empowerment while helping others as you lead through a crisis.

For example, during Hurricane Irma, keeping the main thing the main thing and over-communicating helped me keep the 1,200 people in my shelter calm, orderly, and safe.

When the 2020 COVID-19 global pandemic hit, taking care of my team and myself helped us stay focused on our vision and mission. As we moved through the pandemic, our team met for Monday morning coffee as a check-in, which enabled us to bond and become a more effective team.

As the leader, you set the tone for the people you lead, for your organization, and for your sphere of influence. Therefore, how you respond to a crisis will determine your success.

Remember, it's not a question of if you will find yourself in a crisis. It's a question of when and how you will lead.

EMBRACE cultural diversity for global leadership

By Nadine Binder

Hamburg, Germany

In an era of globalization, digitalization, and worldwide competition, leaders manage diverse teams of senior employees, young talent with experience across various countries, and employees of multi-cultural backgrounds.

Team members might come from working-class or highly educated families, from different regions or varying professional backgrounds. While such cultural diversity can enable creativity and innovation by bringing together additional expertise, perspectives and experience, research has repeatedly shown that diverse teams underperform if leaders cannot create a culture of trust, inclusion, and belonging. Leaders must embrace cultural diversity, acknowledge and appreciate cultural differences, and identify and co-create commonalities to enable meaningful and successful collaboration.

To embrace cultural diversity, leaders need to move beyond traditional notions of culture as fixed, homogeneous entities equated with national cultures toward more dynamic, polyvalent culture models, such as Jürgen Bolten's concept of "fuzzy culture." Bolten favors a multivalent logic of, "both instead of either, or that which reduces cultures to supposedly explanatory binary opposites."

Similar understandings of culture have been proposed.

In recent discussions on transcultural leadership, for example, by Josef Wieland, Julika Baumann Montecinos and colleagues emphasize the need to move beyond acknowledging and accepting differences, to identify and build upon commonalities as a basis for developing shared cultural practices, long-term collaboration, and mutual benefits.

How can leaders adopt such a polyvalent, dynamic understanding of culture and inspire successful collaboration? I propose a model to EMBRACE global leadership. While each letter in EMBRACE represents a key focus area for leaders, EMBRACE reflects the openness and willingness to lead inclusively with,

E - Emotion regulation

No matter how willing leaders are to embrace and appreciate differences, fast-paced, complex environments characterized by uncertainty or ambiguity can leave leaders feeling irritated, frustrated, or overwhelmed. Thus, emotion regulation is essential for leaders, enabling them to manage their initial reactions and create an affective state conducive to reflection and deliberate action. Examples of emotion regulation include practicing mindfulness to observe and identify emotions, and breathing techniques to regulate affective states. A key question for leaders to reflect on is, "What do I feel and what can I learn from this?"

M–Metacognition

Once leaders have successfully regulated their emotional response, metacognition allows them to monitor and regulate cognitive processes. Metacognition invites leaders to take a step back to reflect upon their initial interpretations and assumptions, identify biases, and draw upon relevant cultural knowledge to analyze the situation. Metacognition further entails identifying knowledge gaps and developing strategies to fill those gaps. Key questions that can guide leaders are: What are my assumptions, and how can I move beyond them to better understand the situation? What do I not know, and how can I know?

B–Building trust

As global leaders regulate their emotional and cognitive processes, they can gain and apply their cultural knowledge to build and offer trust as a foundation of long-term, mutually beneficial relationships and collaboration. This requires leaders to attend to the relationship level while acknowledging personal and cultural preferences, affecting how people build and maintain trust. A key question to guide leaders' efforts can be: What does my counterpart need to trust me, and how can I show I trust them?

R–Relational skills

Building upon that initial trust, leaders need strong relational skills to maintain positive relationships within their teams and organizations. While it remains important to acknowledge and accept differences, leaders should actively strive to identify and build upon commonalities for a strong relational foundation and a basis for the co-creation of new commonalities as relationships progress. Key questions for reflection are: How can I make others feel heard, seen, and appreciated? Which commonalities can we discover as we connect deeply and meaningfully with each other?

A–Awareness

While initiating and deepening relationships and collaboration, leaders continuously need high awareness of preferences, perspectives, and biases, both of themselves and others, while acknowledging situational factors and constraints and issues of power and privilege. Key questions to deepen awareness include: What is my perspective, what do I need and want, and what influences my perception? How might others experience this situation, and what do they need and want?

C–Curiosity

Leaders can cultivate a curious mindset guided by an honest interest in understanding themselves and others to promote and deepen awareness and relationships. Authentic curiosity can manifest itself in listening for understanding instead of responding, and noticing premature judgments and actively suspending those to remain curious and open to other perspectives, interpretations, and realities. A key question for leaders to cultivate curiosity can be: What is here for me to learn (about myself, about others, about the situation)?

E–Empathy

Besides curiosity, leaders need cognitive empathy to see how others might experience the situation through perspective-taking. In contrast to affective empathy, cognitive empathy refers to identifying and understanding, rather than experiencing others' emotional experiences. Key reflection questions to support cognitive empathy are: What is the other person feeling? How do they want to be treated, and what do they need right now?

The EMBRACE model offers leaders structure and guidance to widen and deepen their ability to manage culturally diverse teams. The model builds strong relationships by recognizing, accepting, and appreciating differences and commonalities while encouraging the co-creation of new commonalities and ways of being and doing.

References

- Bolten, J. (2014). The Dune Model, in: AFS Intercultural Link, 5b(1), pp. 4-8.
- Wieland, J., & Baumann Montecinos, J. (Eds.) (2019). Transcultural Leadership and Transcultural Competence. Transcultural Management Series, Volume 2. Metropolis.

Become the leader whose feedback is well received

By Kelly Owens, MS, CSCP, LSSGBC

Montgomery, Alabama

To influence your team, become a person whose qualities others respect and admire. When we give feedback to our team members, the goal is to either discontinue undesired behaviors or reinforce desired behaviors. Ultimately, your purpose for the feedback needs to be about their growth, and developing more leaders.

If you do not have the qualities that help you be influential, your feedback will fall flat with the recipient. It will become more about assessing your leadership abilities rather than a personal reflection on your development. A carefully crafted annual review given to employees who see their supervisor as critical, unsupportive, and untrustworthy will not influence any change.

They know you genuinely care

Employees are less likely to feel threatened by feedback provided by someone who genuinely cares about them. It creates a foundation for connecting. I invite you to be strategic in showing you care and go beyond the morning routine of saying hello and asking, "How are you?" in passing.

Take the time to appreciate your team members. Noticing the efforts made by your team can do more than you realize. One reason for the lack of employee engagement is the lack of acknowledgement of what they do. They do not believe what they do matters to anyone. Many people dislike ambiguity. They want to know where they stand and how they are doing. Keep notes about positive things you notice, and share specifically with each team member what you appreciate regularly.

It would be best if you were open to hearing your team's concerns and suggestions. Your team may know more about the details of the daily work than you do, so ask them for their input. Not letting them have a voice leads to frustration. When you ask your team members for their ideas and concerns, this shows you respect their expertise and value them. It invites collaboration, which is a hallmark of high-performance teams.

Embrace being a servant leader.

Servant leaders understand that by supporting their team, everyone wins. Servant leaders find out what their team needs to succeed. Do they need access to resources that could make their job more efficient? Do they need access to training to build the skill sets required? What about helping team members play to their strengths? You will learn these things by listening to your team members. Make sure you listen attentively and follow through on that support. Do not give this lip service.

They can trust you

Trust is written about frequently in leadership articles and books for a good reason. You must develop trust with your team members, or you can forget ever influencing them. Trust requires you to be a person of integrity. They know they can count on you to do what is ethical, moral, and fair. You address issues within the team with equity and objectivity by not playing favorites. You also do not ignore issues. If you ignore problems, the message to the team is they cannot count on you when they need your help in addressing concerns. Ignoring issues leads to resentments because others carry the load due to a team member's poor performance.

Trustworthy leaders manage themselves well at all times. You are consistent. Your team does not have to read you to find out what kind of mood you are in today and if they should avoid you. No one wants to deal with mood swings or someone who cannot put boundaries on personal issues, letting it carry over into the office. Get your insecurities in check. Being transparent about not knowing something is better than arrogantly pretending to know. Leaders who cannot handle their emotions make poor decisions and have interpersonal issues with others.

You lead by example. You continue to grow and develop your competency. The least competent person on the team is the least trusted. Your team wants someone they can go to for mentoring and guidance when new situations arise. They want someone who walks the walk and hardly ever talks the talk.

You help set standards when you lead by example. If you want your team performing at a certain level, you must already perform at that level, or at the least, showing your team you are actively working to reach it yourself. Transparency about areas you are working on shows you value feedback for growth.

You get good at asking questions

As a coach, I can tell you there is power in asking great questions. It helps others to share their perspective and to think about solutions. When we ask open-ended questions, it opens the door to conversation and understanding. You will learn a lot about your team members' critical thinking skills.

Stay focused on questions that start with what, how, when, where, and who. If you ask the why questions, be careful. "Why did you do that?" can lead to self-protective behaviors such as blaming. Instead, you can say, "Help me understand your approach to this situation."

The following simple questions of reflection become coaching for performance in a non-threatening way. Be sure you listen to the responses and continue to ask additional open-ended questions to support more profound introspection.

What worked?

What didn't work?

What would you change?

How would that change make a difference?

What areas do you believe you need to develop?

When you become the leader whose feedback is welcomed, you change the culture of your team. By using regular appreciation and coaching questions, your team values reflection, growth, and development without feeling threatened. Feedback is no longer a list of criticisms. You help eliminate that adage, "You are only as good as your last mistake." Your feedback allows team members to look forward to what they can work on, becoming leaders who care, trust, and who build other future leaders.

Enhancing communication effectiveness—
A perspective from traditional Africa

By Dr. David Thuku

Kenya, Africa

*"To effectively communicate, we must realize that we
are all different in the way we perceive
the world and use this understanding as a guide
to our communication with others."*
- Tony Robbins, American author, coach, speaker,
and philanthropist.

Communication, an integral part of leadership, is contextual.

Within traditional African communities, oral communication was a perfected art passed on from one generation to another. Using stories, metaphors, songs, dances, idioms, expressions and such oral tools integrated within the social-economic model of the communities. This allowed any subject, however complicated or controversial, to surface and be addressed in elegant discourse. Consider, for example, the following traditional story from the Kikuyu community in Kenya.

A long time ago, Hare, Antelope and Hyena were great friends and spent a lot of time together. One day Hyena got caught by a snare set up in a nearby village to catch an antelope to feed a family. Antelope found him hanging upside down in pain and agony, and immediately got to work to free his friend.

Antelope eventually freed Hyena, who had suffered some injuries to his body. Antelope gathered some leaves to apply to Hyena's wounds to help relieve Hyena's pain. As he was doing so, Hyena felt hungry and grabbed Antelope. Hyena explained he was so hungry and wanted to eat Antelope. Antelope felt surprised and started pleading with Hyena not to eat him, explaining that it would be unfair considering that moments earlier he rescued Hyena from a man's snare.

Just then, their mutual friend Hare appeared and found them arguing. Hare offered to arbitrate the matter and asked each of them to explain what had happened. After listening to both of them, he requested they retrace the entire scene to get a clearer perspective, to assist him in making a fair judgment. Hare and Antelope, therefore, hoisted Hyena back into the snare as Antelope had initially found him. When Hyena was finally hanging upside down on the snare, Hare said he was ready to give his verdict.

"You should never repay good with evil," he told Hyena. "Our friend Antelope saved you, but now you want to eat him." And with that, Hare and Antelope left Hyena trapped as they went away laughing at him.

The above story, one of the many stories told to us as we grew up in the village, weaved several themes together. It captured the reality of competing interests of various stakeholders within our ecosystems, the wisdom of sometimes elevating the common good while subordinating personal interests, trust within teams, and not always taking matters at face value.

I have fond memories of us sitting around the fireplace listening to our grandparents narrating captivating traditional stories in the evenings. In retrospect, I realized that we got to learn a lot as part of being prepared for the life ahead of us. The content we covered included concepts in natural sciences, sociology, philosophy, divinity, anthropology, commerce, history and many other subjects without ascribing such specific names to the content. Our storytellers would not, for example, tell us they were teaching us how to influence the behavior of people around us. They would tell us stories that integrated the teaching.

We did not take any written notes as we listened to the stories. The entertaining component of the story made it stick in our memories, embedding the key learning into our subconscious. The richness of the finessed oral skills compensates for the lack of written accounts in traditional African communities. Though the stories and other traditional practices have appeared like simplistic and disjointed activities at face value, I came to appreciate that they were part of an integrated socio-economic model not captured in literary records.

I consider myself privileged to have had a taste of the two worlds—the power of the written word and the potency of the oral medium of instruction. Born around the period of transition from colonial Africa to post-colonial Africa, I enjoyed the benefit of hearing first-hand oral accounts of how traditional Africa was from my grandparents' generation. In addition, I had first-hand experience of residue aspects of traditional Africa's socio-economic model that had survived the significant mutation during colonization.

My paternal grandfather, who could neither read nor write, was a traditional knowledge and practice custodian. They entrusted him with the oral transmission of knowledge, values and cultural practices to children as they graduated from childhood to adulthood through the traditional rite of passage. My father later enrolled me in the contemporary education system, where I got exposed to the power of the written word and the structure of knowledge into various disciplines. My double exposure to the two worlds colors my perspective of the world today.

Using stories and other oral tools enhances communication as they allow people to venture into complex or taboo subjects to enhance effective communication. It is one potent tool the contemporary world can borrow from traditional Africa to aid effective communication within teams and communities. Though today's stories are unlikely to be about antelopes, hares and hyenas that engage in human-like activities, refined storytelling skills are a great tool to have in one's management and leadership toolbox.

Mentorship

Lead by example
Keeping your word = Your success
in sales and business

By Joe Pici
Featured author
Orlando, Florida

The power of keeping your word is an intangible force that will give you a competitive edge. Although it costs you nothing, it might have a great impact on your success and increase your bottom line. It will also help you attract and keep quality clients and earn you qualified referrals. You don't have to spend money on training to learn how to keep your word, but it can boost your success to the next level.

There was a time in history when a person's handshake was their bond—they agreed over a table, and it was binding. If a person gave their word, it was as good as a contract.

Are you good at keeping your word?

Do you always do what you say you're going to do when you say you're going to do it? Do you have the code and character that your word is your bond?

In today's world, many people struggle with keeping their word. You hear someone say, "I'll be there," or, "I'll call you," or, "I'll get you that proposal." But then it doesn't happen. I've had multiple clients express their surprise over how I follow through, exclaiming, "You did what you said you were going to do!"

One day, I got on the phone to follow up with a high-profile attorney about training. He said, "You told me your proposal would be in my inbox when I woke up, and I found that, sure enough, your proposal had come through at 3:45 a.m. You're a man who is good at keeping your word." Why is that now so uncommon? What has happened to our integrity? Why has situational ethics taken prevalence over pure ethics?

I don't have an answer to those questions, but I can tell you this: keeping your word will help you stand out from your competitors. You will become known as a person who understands that the word "client" originally meant "under the protection of." As you protect your clients, ensuring that they receive excellent service, your reputation as a person of integrity will build your business as nothing else can.

What is at the core of keeping your word?

The New York City Marathon is a world-renowned event. One year as the first runners were crossing the finish line, the media rushed to interview the record-setting winner. They all wanted to know his story. He said, "I'm not your story. The real story is the guy who will finish three hours behind me. The crowd will be gone, with no one to cheer for anymore. He will run his quiet race and finish because he said he was going to."

"Who is he?" asked a reporter. Replied the winner, "His name is CHARACTER."

Character is at the core of keeping your word and is vital to your ability to overcome adversity.

Most of us have a concept of integrity. It can mean honest and morally upright or structurally sound. When applied to a person, it can also mean that they consistently follow up their words with action. In life, what people say and what they do rarely match. I'm looking for people whose words and actions match. But before I can look for people like that, I have to be that person. I must deliver on time, on scope, on budget, without changing the rules.

Keeping your word with integrity costs you nothing, but not keeping it can cost you everything. Learning to keep your word requires a change in your perspective or your attitude. You should evaluate your words before you speak.

Unfortunately, in today's culture, commitments are not kept. When a person says, "I will be there," what they mean is, "I will be there unless (insert extenuating circumstance)." Rather than sticking to their commitments, they give themselves too much slack. Yes, there are genuine circumstances that prevent you from keeping your word, but they should be infrequent, never a pattern.

My challenge to you

Consider the benefits of keeping your word. You will gain an unfair advantage over your competition because many people don't weigh their words before they speak and rarely follow through.

Remember Aesop's fable about the boy who cried wolf? The truth of that story is that no one believes a liar even when they're telling the truth. If you say you're going to do something and then don't do it, you have told a lie. If this happens enough, even if you are known to keep your word, you lose the trust and confidence of others, possibly at significant cost to yourself.

Learn to keep your word with integrity, and you will earn the respect and trust of others. Your word is the bedrock of all your interactions with people, and it should be your bond. When you have established yourself as someone who always does what you say you'll do, you'll find yourself well along your path to success.

Building a team

By Eric Bibel

San Diego, California

Those whom you surround yourself with will dictate the direction of your organization. Choose wisely.

I have had the opportunity to build multiple teams throughout my lending career, and I have identified a few key attributes to consider when deciding to build or expand one's organizational footprint. One of them is building a team. Without the support of a solid team, a team that enables a leader to honor commitments made to clients and referral partners, your organization will fail.

The word team is thrown around lightly, in the sense that one simply assembles a group of people to get a job done and slap a brand on it. This is the farthest from the actual outcome. To create a lasting brand, and an organization with a buy-in from everyone, we must ensure that those brought onboard are the right people placed in the right positions.

This starts with breaking down the sales process and identifying what roles need to be filled. My partners and I created a process to identify where these individual candidates can be found and then laid out a concise hiring model. This included an assessment test for each candidate.

Once a panel of members receive the assessment, a round of panel interviews are administered. Interview questions are tailored to the role, as well as specific charter questions identified in the assessment. The interview typically lasts between 45 minutes to one hour. Upon completion of the interview, the panel then compares notes and decides on the next steps. For the candidate to be considered, there needs to be a unanimous decision among the members. After the meeting, a telephone call is placed to the candidate to advise on the next steps.

In the second and final interview, the candidate is then given a concise breakdown of the job roles, core values of the organization, and a concise outline of expectations. Any doubt around what is expected of them is addressed on day one. Unspoken expectations yield no positive outcome.

Once the job offer is extended, the team then sets in motion the playbook for the next 30, 60, to 90 days and beyond for the new team member. This process includes specific milestones the new team member must accomplish within those time windows. Check-ins are administered bi-weekly followed with a report to ensure the individual is on target. In addition, the leader checks in for a monthly recap. This process provides a tremendous lift in our hiring and onboarding process; however, it is not the end for the continued development of the team ethos. This process is ongoing and requires an incredibly strong foundation of core values and buy-in from all involved.

Core values have been an integral pillar in teams I have been a part of or have had a hand in creating. This process drives decision-making and ensures that forward progress aligns with those values. These are created based on team input, and hard copies are placed throughout our office, on desks, and on our website. When decisions are processed, the question asked among the group is always, "Does the potential outcome align with our core values?" If the answer is yes, then we proceed forward. If it does not align, then we pull back and return to the drawing board.

A solid team can be your propellant in business ventures. The opposite is true as well with misalignment of the team causing the demise of the organization. The upkeep is always on the forefront as markets are always changing. Holding true to your core values and surrounding yourself with people that share in the same mindset will always ensure your continued growth and success. As markets shift, this strong foundation will enable the group to adapt and thrive in any changing atmosphere.

Harness your aggression

By Brian Brogen
Mulberry, Florida

I entered the construction industry immediately after working one summer as a stockman in a grocery store. My first role as a 17-year-old was as a shipping clerk and "gopher." Because of insurance restrictions, they did not permit me to operate or be around heavy equipment. However, I had a driver's license and was ready to "go for" this and "go for" that. They sent me to get a much-needed tool or materials required to complete a project.

When I turned 18, I was eager and finally allowed to work with the other adults around the noisy and powerful construction equipment. I wanted to show my capability to produce alongside some weathered and hardened construction craftsmen.

One of my first opportunities to "pull my weight" and "earn my stripes" was on a crew assembling industrial conveyors; we were attaching large rolling idlers to big steel frames with huge bolts and massive wrenches. It was fascinating and rewarding to see parts and pieces assembled into working machinery.

I was full of zeal and vigor to be a productive team member and graduate from gopher to craftsman. One day, we needed a tool to continue our assembly work and remain productive. As a former gopher I knew what supply house had the tool we needed, and I was familiar with procuring this tool.

I jumped into making it happen. I signed out the company truck, drove to the supply house, picked up the tool we needed, and raced back to keep the crew productive. I was expecting a hero's welcome. When I returned an hour later with the problem solved, much to my chagrin, a perturbed supervisor who wanted to know my whereabouts met me, and asked me who I thought I was? He then told me the big boss wanted to see me. Uh oh! What had I done?

I headed to the office, and on the way, I had a knot in my stomach I used to have on my frequent visits to the principal's office during my troubled school years.

I sheepishly entered the office. The big boss had questions about where I had been and why I had left the site without the supervisor's permission. I explained why I had taken these actions. While he understood my motives, he informed me of company policies and procedures, and how the supervisor is responsible for the crew and their needs and to know where they are and what they are doing.

He instructed me to get permission before leaving the worksite in the future.

Then he encouraged me with these words. "Brian, you are an aggressive person by nature, but you must harness that aggression and use it purposefully and thoughtfully."

I have now encouraged countless other individuals with this simple message to, "Harness your aggression."

Over the years, I have learned that unharnessed aggression leads to destroyed relationships in careers, friendships, and family.

Thankfully, the big boss was a wise leader and knew how to deliver a correction message and soften the blow by recognizing potential, and not smothering my desire to be a productive team member. This mentor has been a confidant and staunch supporter of mine for a few decades now.

A great mentor knows how to hold others accountable, recognizes their potential, sees their strengths, and encourages them to be the best version of themselves. I have had many mentors and would not be where I am today without their guidance and encouragement.

As Stan Toler says in the book *Minute motivators for leaders,* "Every leader should be a mentor, but every leader should have a mentor."

Values of a mentor

They are patient. Mentors understand their mentees need time to develop. You can't train experience; you gain experience through action and trial and error.

They communicate well. Mentors are excellent listeners and seek to understand the mentee's needs.

They are models of leadership. Mentors set the example. They aren't perfect, but they know that others follow them and mirror their actions.

They come to where you are. Mentors can recognize where another person is, and get on their level to communicate with them and bring them to the desired outcome.

They recognize potential. Mentors see the potential in an individual. They recognize their strengths and guide that individual to their fullest potential.

I will challenge you as a leader and a mentor to add value to others as their mentor, reach your hand out and challenge them. We can create a chain of mentorship and make the world a better place. With the parts and pieces that assemble a working piece of machinery, we can come together as a community and create a better society.

Voices of leadership: Developing high-performance leaders

By Carlos Cody

Hampton, Georgia

Section 1: Know yourself to grow yourself

> *"Leaders need to embrace and master the art of transformation for their organizations to thrive."*
> - Steven J. Bowen.

All great leadership begins with self first. Until you can lead yourself well, you cannot lead others well. To embark on the journey of growing yourself, you need to first have a quick self-assessment. The easiest way to get a quick overview is for you to take a personality assessment.

Once you have completed the assessment, ask, "What did you find out about yourself?" The test will help you analyze your strengths, weaknesses and develop a roadmap of how you can transform into the leader you desire. The assessment is good, but it is not the be-all, see-all for you. Remember, you are unique, and this assessment is only the starting point of your growth.

Realize that there will always be limitations.

The good news is that you develop your influence to always have stronger leaders around you to help cover some of your limitations. From this assessment, you will work to create a vision for yourself, a plan of how to become the best version of yourself, and this will serve as your growth roadmap to enhance your career.

Section 2: The beginning stages of leading

"Leaders instill in their people a hope for success and a belief in themselves. Positive leaders empower people to accomplish their goals."
- Unknown.

Learning about yourself is vital to being able to lead others. You need to know your tendencies to create self-awareness of how others perceive you.

You need self-awareness to develop influence with your team members. Developing influence and trust is the only way you can lead others. How you can develop trust and influence is by serving others and by investing time in others.

To maximize the investment of time and service, you will take your future leaders through a similar process you have gone through to develop yourself, as in Section 1. You will take them through the personality assessment to gain quick insights into how others are, their strengths, weaknesses, and tendencies. This assessment will help you understand how to talk to someone, help you understand how they process information, and help you position them in the organization.

From here, you take the time now through one one-on-ones to work on their growth plan and career plan. To develop deep influence and trust, make sure the plan encompasses growth outside of work as well. Remember, leadership development at its core is character development. As you are leading others, you are helping them reach their potential while growing them as a person. Here is where you help a person develop vision, values, and a roadmap to what they define as success.

Once you have the roadmap they have created, it will be essential to hold them to their standard as a coach, mentor, and sponsor when they exceed expectations. You serve as a coach helping to course correct when they are veering from their goals, a coach that must hold others accountable and show others the way to improvement. You are a coach that must continue to stretch others, not allowing comfort to steal progress.

You will be a mentor guiding them with viable wisdom and key information to help them grow, a mentor that helps them navigate their career and continue to progress. You will be a mentor who must listen effectively and ask questions to help them solve their own problems. Last, you will also be a sponsor for them when they have met and exceeded your expectations, raising them up as a leader ready for the next level.

Remember, when you start the journey of developing others, you are not in it to keep people, but to elevate them. If you are truly developing others, you must also be willing to let them move on when the time comes. Therefore, developing and leading others is a leader's primary job. Always be building your leadership bench. You should see yourself as a leadership factory constantly developing others into the best version of who they choose to be.

Section 3: Building a high-performance team

"Grow the leader and you grow the organization."
- John Maxwell.

In any business, the leader will dictate the lid of that organization. Your leaders will determine your success when you are running your function, department, business unit, and organization. Your primary duty in building a high-performance team is to identify and develop leaders. The higher you go, the more removed you can become and the more you will have to work through others to accomplish business objectives. Your goal is to increase the output of your organization and the output of cross-functional teams that will benefit from your leadership.

Low-level team performance happens when you increase the rate at which you perform activities. Mid-level performance is when you leverage others and delegate effectively the things you do. High-performance is when you develop leaders who can carry your vision and develop others to do the same, leaving you to focus on high-level activities. When building high-performance teams, a leader's foundational keys are a strong character, a hunger for learning, and commitment to becoming competent in their role. If the potential leader has these, then you look for their leadership potential. Grade your potential leader in the following areas: People skills, planning and strategic thinking, vision, and ability to deliver results. Remember, you may only focus on a select few, but those select few will lead and affect 100's to 1,000's of other team members.

If those leaders pass the test, you must now begin training them in leadership development and on the skills of not only delivering results but also on over delivery. In business, they hire you to deliver a result, and your leaders must know how to develop teams that can execute together.

By focusing your energy on continuous improvement by growing and developing your people, you will create a culture that creates the environment for a high-performance team to emerge.

Never forget that, "Everything rises and falls on leadership." - John Maxwell.

Leadership

By Brian Covey

Nashville, Tennessee

L eadership is something you develop; as much as we wish we could open up a manual and instantly become qualified to lead. It's a process. There's no reason to do it alone. Books like this can give you the edge, the boost, and the knowledge to advance quicker.

For example, you can't read a book on abdominal workouts and instantly have a six-pack, but you can take that knowledge and get to work. It's a daily devotional practice. I believe you can do it.

I could teach you many things, but I want to talk about three key elements.

To excel today, we need virtual and in-personal hybrid skills.

Virtual chitchat needs to come to a 0 point stop

- First, take an audit of your typical meeting style. Do you talk about the weather for the first five minutes? Do you enjoy that, or are you frustrated? The person on the other side of the line feels similar. In the next few weeks, practice this phrase, "Are you alright if we dive right into today's topic? I want to give you the support you need."

- Next, work on making your 60 minute meetings into 30 minute meetings by looking for wasted time. Turn 30 minutes into 15 minutes.

- Last, switch about 50% of your video calls to phone calls so you can get in some physical exercise, perform minor tasks and reduce screen fatigue.

Virtual rounding needs to be implemented in your calendar

- I can't physically telephone my entire loanDepot team daily or even throughout the week. What I can do is post on social media, so I'm omnipresent, represent my values and comment on their posts. Their family has a higher approval rating of me when they see me celebrating their five-year-old's birthday in the comments, as an example. I spend two hours a day doing this type of connection work, and while I've outsourced posting, this specific engagement fills my tank.

In-person bonding, scheduled at least once a year, is vital for maintenance

- Plan to meet your clients, team members and executives at least once per year; otherwise, the deep work you are doing, now that you've eliminated small talk, may not leave the deep interpersonal connection you need for longevity of your relationships.

Your team needs to see you being your best: Who is that, and how can you show them?

- Last, take some time to implement the best boundaries practices to motivate your team and colleagues. I post my gym time workout every day on social media, and my team has reflected this to me, saying, "I know if you had time to get a workout, I do too."

The ability to coach hard and to be coached is not a luxury, but a necessity

I was pushing hard for my team to grow, and they met me with a lot of resistance. I'm a nice guy, but business is business, and I will do everything not to let a team member or my company fail. In my mind, "Let's have this awkward push and grow moment now, so you have a paycheck later."

I would use this exercise in your journal, notes app, etc. every day to grow and to help others succeed.

Four questions for the inward and outward approach (use daily)

Where are you weak and overwhelmed?

Who do you know that isn't feeling the same way?

Where are you excelling right now?

Who do you know that isn't feeling the same way?

Once you've filled out the questions, ask for help.

Go live on social or call a friend who is struggling and give back.

Adapt to change by intentionally changing every day

Leadership is muscle grown. A significant shift you can make so change doesn't destroy you or your mindset, is to change a bit every day: A podcast here, training there, a retreat etc.

By changing yourself you'll become a better example to your team, who will mirror your ability to adapt and survive, even in challenging times as we saw in 2020 and early 2021.

The following are a few ways I adapt to changing my situation.

1. I changed my mindset around failure. Failure empowers me; I don't seek it out. But, when something happens that others construe as unfavorable, I ask myself, "Ok, what did I learn? How will I refuse to repeat this, and who can I teach this lesson to?"

2. I remembered I am a mirror for my family and team. The way I show myself handling stress is how they will. I ask myself, "Is this the legacy you want to leave, Brian?"

3. I pour into my network. My network is my net worth. It is vital, and I commit to it and service and learn from my peers every day.

Implementing these quick but effective practices will change your life if you take the time to do the work, change your current ways, and lead by example. I am excited to see your evolution. I can't wait to chat on social media with you and hear about how these worked for you!

Let's go!

The art of transitioning leadership style

By Sean Gibson
Orlando, Florida

arly in my career, I felt privileged to work with a former US Air Force fighter pilot trained in surveillance and in choosing the best course of action if a situation became hostile. Through his example, I learned of a concept known as Situational Awareness.

When we collaborated for sales meetings, we pre-planned our course of action and agreed on our main discussion points. Entering the boardroom, he would look around to observe and evaluate the situation. I knew he was assessing the people and what they were doing. Because of this skill set, he picked up on the subtle needs of the clients. He then decisively provided a solution that met their expectations and benefited our sales organization.

While it is easy to understand the need for Situational Awareness, especially in choosing the right leadership style for a group, the real challenge comes in knowing what to look for, and then knowing how to assimilate that information into a functional solution. This chapter will discuss assessing the "situations" of those we lead and use this intel to foster the right workplace environment. It all begins with observing the ethos and ethics of your group.

Although I won't give a complete etymology of the word "ethos," it helps to understand its origin and what it has morphed into today. The word ethos describes a people group's customs, character, and habits. Over time, a secondary word developed from ethos; the word is "ethikos," or as we now know it, ethics. When we talk about ethics, we define that group's moral rules and beliefs.

Ethos describes the what and how of a group in today's terms. Ethics helps us understand the WHY for the behavior of that same group. Let's go a step further and learn to distinguish both the ethos and ethics of a group by looking at an example we all have encountered in everyday life.

Suppose you have ever been around an older friend or family member born in the early 1900s. They say things like, "Back in my day, we used to get up early and…" followed by a rant sounding something like, "People today don't know how to work as our generation used to." As we listen to them innocently brag about how much stronger they were physically compared to how we are now, we agree that there is some truth to it.

For many, the ethos that generation lived under involved getting up early and performing tasks that we now consider hard manual labor. They got the job done from never-ending farm work to maintaining and fixing the tools and equipment; that generation used daylight to be productive.

During that same time, when someone would observe a young man or young woman diligently at work, they would say that, "They have a good work ethic," meaning they not only knew what and how to perform a job, but also understood the big picture of why they were doing it.

If a young farm girl didn't get up early to milk the cows and retrieve the eggs from the hens, her mom would not have the supplies needed to make the big breakfast that her husband and sons would require to work a full day on the farm.

After breakfast, the men would get to work in the fields, tending to the crops and making sure that the harvest would be healthy and bountiful, not only out of a sense of duty but also out of moral obligation. If they didn't do their part, the family could lose out on the profits of a successful harvest, not to mention having less seed to plant for the next season and less food to consume. Everyone had their part to play, and they believed that wholeheartedly.

When we observe the ethos and ethics dynamic of today's working culture, we see fewer manual labor roles and more knowledge-based positions. Despite the difference in our work environments, we still have a way of doing things and reasons and beliefs about what we do. Today, we call those reasons and beliefs a work culture, but ethics is still deep down.

Using our situational awareness with those we lead gives us a chance to understand the ethos and ethics of whom we are leading. As wise leaders, we need to understand the workers and their jobs, and why their work is vital to them and the company. This information will provide us with the insights required to lead and guide our group.

Regrettably, too many leaders cannot understand their workers' current situation, their jobs (ethos) and current workplace beliefs (ethic). To make matters worse, out of touch leaders devour leadership theories and fads, and then rush these new insights to their people without considering if it is compatible with their current ethos and group ethics.

When a new leadership style is required, it is best not to rush things or change too much at once. Like my friend used to say, "Slow is smooth, and smooth is fast."

As a good leader, embrace and emphasize a few of the best practices (ethos) used in the workplace before subtly adjusting or adding new leadership concepts to the group. Doing this gradually will reinforce the belief (ethic) that your employees are vital, valued, and understood.

It will position them to be more receptive to your desired leadership style changes.

Mentoring: The key to long-term success

By Bill Mason
Destin, Florida

Slingshot to success

I have always admired great leaders like C. S. Lewis, General George Patton, Steve Jobs, Warren Buffett, and Elon Musk. They have inspired me, and I've read about their lives and leadership styles, but they are not the men who mentored me and helped me become the leader I am today.

Cecil Bean, David Coffield, Dave Mead, and Jim Downing have had the most significant impact. They are probably unknown to you. Thanks to them, my life has been transformed. My mentors acted like guides and have helped me grow in my leadership skills. The unseen professionals of everyday life make significant contributions to the world. Those whose lives they affect are the ones who know about their gift.

When I was a young Army warrant officer and Blackhawk pilot, I admired Cecil Bean. The intentional way he invested in the junior leaders was astounding. Because I saw how he had changed their lives, I took a risk and asked him to invest in me. He accepted. We would meet for breakfast at 6:30 in the morning, his only time available. He transformed my life, and I paid the price to meet with him when his schedule allowed. Cecil's impact has led me to ask other men I respect to continue to mentor me on my 40 year leadership journey. As if rocket fuel were propelling me around the moon, they have been my rocket fuel to supercharge my leadership journey.

Qualities of a mentor

Mentors have a profound effect on you. That's why it's so important to choose the right mentor. Be selective in whom you choose to mentor. A mentor's character is as important as their abilities. Look for excellence in these areas when selecting a mentor.

Work excellence

Do they work well and lead well? How well are they respected in their fields and communities? We seek mentorship to benefit from their expertise. New businesses need mentors. Over 90% of newly founded companies fail in the first year, and only 10% succeed. When businesses find mentors in their field, this number changes, seeing a success rate of up to 90%. This is a power mentorship.

Home life

Are they capable of being excellent parents and partners? Many leaders excel in their careers but struggle in other areas. If I am looking for a mentor, I look at their spouses and children to see how they react. Work is essential, but relationships are also crucial. Not investing more in their closest relationships is one of the top regrets people list at the end of their lives. Carve out time for them. Start with your big rocks. Ensure that you schedule time every week, month, and year for your spouse, children, mentor, and dearest friends.

Life on life

Are they willing to live life together? Mentoring is about building relationships, so only talking about leading is not enough. Influential mentors pour themselves into those they mentor. Mentoring is more of an art than a science. Although my influential mentors taught me career-related techniques, tactics, and procedures, their most significant contributions have been in other areas. We spend time together. We work out, help each other with home projects, play golf, go to the beach, have family dinners, and go on trips. We had some of our most memorable mentoring moments during long road trips, during which we talked for hours. Despite not having a schedule or topic, the discussion was rich and transformational. When building long-term relationships, vulnerability is required, leading to robust growth.

Courageous

Mentors must be courageous. They must have the courage to be a capable leader. Be clear about boundaries and guidelines in your relationship. This is setting expectations. Mentors are courageous enough to ask hard questions and challenge preconceived ideas. They give you courage in times of struggle, weakness, or trouble. They will lift your spirits and make you believe you are more than your failures. Courage is holding yourself and others to high standards. It is giving grace (getting what you do not deserve), at the right time, for the right reason. When I am at my wits' end, they know when to kick me in the pants and give a kind word.

Next steps and challenge

Mentoring is a time-consuming process. When I first heard Jim Downing, a Pearl Harbor Veteran, speak about mentoring, his character-building philosophy captured my imagination. By teaching once a week, he believed you could pass on knowledge. To go deeper, you pass on skills, which take you to the next level of training. Ideally, by meeting two to three times a week, using guided experience, you can accomplish next level training. If you want another person to inherit your character, you must meet with them four to seven times a week. It is this enormous investment of time that is important. You must teach, train, and lead by example to pass on your best qualities. Character is much more caught than taught.

The challenge for you this week is to find at least one person to challenge, encourage, invest, and pour into your life. Mentors are out there—look for them. You do not have a mentor because you do not ask. Don't delay; find your mentor today.

Values-based leadership:
Leading with influence

By Sheryl Mays

Orlando, Florida

Leading with influence is an act of great leadership. Thought leaders might call it a requirement. Spiritual leaders call it an assignment. I believe it's an ability to empower others. My mentor Rick says, "Leaders are to get better, help others get better, and then get better at helping others get better." Rick and I have had sessions where we talked about the purpose of leaders.

As a leader, when you seek continuous improvement through self-reflection, you can ask for continuous improvement by empowering others; because you see something in them they might not yet see in themselves.

Let's visit William Shakespeare, where he wrote, "Uneasy is the head that wears a crown," from *Henry IV*. Today we phrase it as, "Heavy is the head that wears the crown." The basic meaning refers to those charged with major responsibility carrying a heavy burden that makes it difficult to relax. (From the website No Sweat Shakespeare.)

In the Shakespearean play, the king is complaining about his inability to sleep as war approaches. Ordinary people, or those with the fortune of having no cares, get a good night's sleep. But the king, with all his comforts, is denied sleep. He is a king and has to take responsibility for what happens, which keeps him awake at night.

As a leader, are you staying awake at night surfing your mental data banks about your team's goals or your company's objectives? Are you wondering how you will make it through four quarters, keeping all plates in the air and focusing on an important factor that, "We must make a profit." Even amid disruption, yes, you must still make a profit. That, my friend, is enough to make you lose sleep.

Many leaders don't make time for self-reflection because they wear that crown Shakespeare referenced. I'd like to share another line, "Easy lies the head that empowers others." To continuously improve as a leader, review your development, understand human behavior, and communicate more effectively with others. Self-reflection is a powerful assessment an individual has for their continued growth. It is the ability to look inward and identify what you stand for, identify your values, and where you need improvement. When we understand and embrace our experiences, we can empower others to use their talents. When taking an internal audit, you know what it's like to witness the extraordinary in others. You use this ability to see something special that needs to be birthed in someone they haven't seen in themselves yet. You can be influential because you are helping others grow by providing opportunities.

Here's how I'll sum up this article. In 1996, I began my career in the non-profit sector. I served as a receptionist for the Make-A-Wish Foundation of Central Florida. I met my first mentor, Robert, at that time. Robert was a laid-back executive. He would come in with his dog on some days, he would wear his baseball cap backwards and walk through the office, or would share a funny story about an encounter at a meeting. Robert would enlist or volunteer someone for an assignment that he could do. He knew he needed to strengthen his team of players. For our benefit, Robert trusted us to fulfill the company's objectives. He was an influential leader that empowered everyone in the office. No one felt marginalized in their role. We were all important to the organization.

In my second year, Robert and I would discuss my future and where I wanted to take my career. I knew I wanted to take on a much larger role at the organization. Still, I wasn't ready to sit in boardrooms as a representative or meet with a major donor, or even speak on behalf of the organization. The Make-A-Wish Foundation has a national presence, and who am I to speak on its behalf? So, I listed everything I would need to develop, such as my confidence, writing proposals, managing volunteer committees, and fundraising. I presented this list to Robert, and he immediately began mapping out ways and opportunities for me to grow.

I began speaking in small groups, raising small amounts of money, eating lunch with him and a donor, taking classes on stewardship, and joining Toastmasters. Then in 1999, I became the Assistant Director of Development. I revisited those days frequently as I ascended in my career to land a gig as VP of Admissions. For the next six plus years, I led high-performing teams across 25 campuses throughout the country.

What's the lesson here? According to the O'Reilly website, best known for helping tech teams stay ahead, values-based leadership works by word, action, and example. Values-based leaders seek to inspire and motivate, using their influence to pursue what matters. What matters, of course, depends somewhat on choice.

Some decide what matters is attaining a particular job title or salary level, or perhaps a bigger house or a vacation home, or a luxury car. For values-based leaders, what matters is the greater good, the positive change within a team, department, division, or organization.

When you decide to wear that crown that you so earnestly deserve, remember the words of my mentor Rick, "Leaders are to get better, help others get better and then get better at helping others get better." As a leader, when you ask for one more degree, you will remember… Your influence is through your ability to bring others to the peaks of their talents.

Learn to empower.

The leadership lift

By Dr. Kelvin McCree

Lakeland, Florida

By now, you've likely heard about the Tampa Bay Buccaneers Super Bowl LV win over the Kansas City Chiefs. Being a resident of the Tampa Bay area, this has been a long time coming. While the Buccaneers won the 2002—2003 Super Bowl after many years of being the laughing stock of football, they had not reached the playoffs since 2007. So, you can imagine for us here in Tampa Bay, this win is the equivalent of winning the billion-dollar lottery Powerball.

But the question many people are rhetorically asking is, "What was the difference this year?" It's rhetorical because we know the answer to that question? You guessed it, Tom Brady. That got me thinking about organizations and the leaders who influence them.

After an unceremonious exit from the only team he'd played for since entering the NFL, Tom Brady landed with the Bucs and immediately began drawing from a talent list of players. Only a year after retiring from the NFL, he coaxed tight end Rob Gronkowski out of retirement. Gronk replied to Brady, "I've been waiting on you to call." Brady also tapped running back Leonard Fournette, who himself was out of a job, after the Jacksonville Jaguars released him. And one startling choice Brady tapped was Antonio Brown, who, like Schleprock in the Flintstones cartoon, trouble never seemed far behind him.

What do Gronkowski, Fournette and Brown have in common? None were with the Buccaneers the year before. There are some incredible lessons organizations can learn from the moves made by Tom Brady.

Great leaders draw great people

Many leaders spend a great deal of time simply working to achieve results. While results matter, they are not the Holy Grail. Great leaders take it a step further and draw great people to build a great culture, and are never satisfied with what they have. Great leaders also have an influence that causes others to want to be around them.

Tom Brady knew Gronkowski still had more juice. Brady knew Leonard Fournette could still be a punishing runner. Brady knew that with the right mentoring, Antonio Brown could flourish. And because of Tom Brady's leadership, not only did the men he recruited excel, they were the keys to the four Buccaneer touchdowns in the Super Bowl game.

Who is your Tom Brady in your organization? Who is that person in your organization that uses their influence to draw out the best in others, the one person inside or outside of your organization you want to work for you?

Great leaders are lifters

You've likely heard the phrase, "Rising tides lift all ships." While we associate this aphorism with economic policy, I believe the idea of a rising tide lifts all ships applies to outstanding leaders and how they influence others. When leaders understand that their influence links them to becoming progressively better, they believe it can only cause others to rise when they are rising.

Brady, at age 44, is still getting up early, still studying film and still learning, despite having little else to prove on the field. He is the GOAT, but he knows great leaders continue to learn, and learners become lifters.

How can you be like Tom Brady (and still be you)?

1. Spend a little time each week looking for great people to invest in or mentor.

2. Develop people to become something instead of getting them to do something.

3. Make connections and keep notes on the talent tap down the road.

4. Instead of putting together a list of potential candidates to replace Susie when she gets promoted or moves on, have your list of people who are the type of talent you want now.

I believe we all want to be around or work for great leaders. I know that neither you nor I am Tom Brady; however, we can certainly make sure we're the person others would want to follow.

So, I leave you with the question I started with: Who's your Tom Brady?

Acknowledgements

This book is a reality thanks to many people who believed in me and bought into the vision I have for creating a community of leaders to share their voice with the world.

Carolyn Flower is the CEO of Oxygen Publishing Agency, the publisher of this book. Carolyn was the first person to hear my vision and encouraged me about the potential of creating a book series. She also made me aware of the real challenges associated with a collaboration book. Carolyn and the team at Oxygen Publishing have been amazing to work with and have helped me to meet the challenges associated with this project.

Our featured authors for Volume One of *Voices For Leadership* took a risk and shared their name and notoriety with me before there were any contributing authors signed up. Thanks for having faith in me and joining us on this project. In particular, Eileen McDargh was an early advocate and gave me ideas to make the book and community better. Thank you Eileen, for your continued support and encouragement.

Our contributing authors have invested in this book and shared their voice with the readers. Thanks for becoming founding members of this worldwide growing community, the best is yet to come.

About the Author

Brian Brogen is a coach, trainer, and speaker with an emphasis on communication and team building. As a certified human behavior expert, Brian has a knack for developing teams and individuals personally and professionally. Brian works with organizations and individuals, coaching, and training using his experience, knowledge, tenacity, and sense of humor. Brian is the best-selling author of *The 100-Hour Pilot*. Brian enjoys flying with friends and family as a hobby.

Find out more about Brian and the services he provides
at www.buildcs.net

Would you like to join the Voices For Leadership community?
Connect with us: www.voicesforleadership.com

CPSIA information can be obtained
at www.ICGtesting.com
Printed in the USA
LVHW082156160322
713503LV00037B/8

9 781990 093395